WITNESS
TO THE
CIVIL WAR

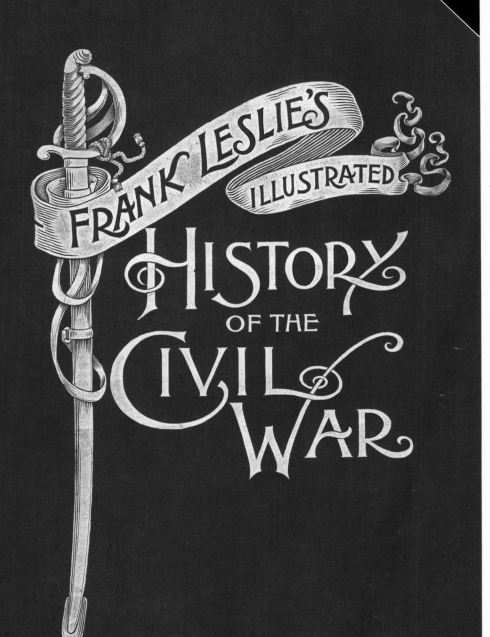

FRANK LESLIE'S

ILLUSTRATED

History

OF THE

Civil

War

WITNESS
TO THE
CIVIL WAR

First-Hand Accounts from
Frank Leslie's Illustrated Newspaper

COMPILED BY J.G. LEWIN AND P.J. HUFF
EDITED BY STUART A.P. MURRAY

FOREWORD BY JAMES G. BARBER,
HISTORIAN, NATIONAL PORTRAIT GALLERY

Collins
An Imprint of HarperCollinsPublishers

HarperCollins books may be purchased for educational, business, or sales promotional use. For information please write: Special Markets Department, HarperCollins Publishers, Inc., 10 East 53rd Street, New York, NY 10022.

Produced for HarperCollins by:

Hydra Publishing
129 Main Street
Irvington, NY 10533
www.hylaspublishing.com

FIRST EDITION

The name of the "Smithsonian," "Smithsonian Institution," and the sunburst logo are registered trademarks of the Smithsonian Institution.

Library of Congress Cataloging-in-Publication Data has been applied for.

ISBN-10: 0-06-089150-5
ISBN-13: 978-0-06-089150-3

06 07 08 09 10   10 9 8 7 6 5 4 3 2 1

FOREWORD

When English-born Frank Leslie launched his popular illustrated newspaper in 1855 he was desperately trying to establish himself in America as a journalist and publisher. His vision for a newspaper that was largely pictorial in content was truly modern, especially in an age before the use of photography was technologically possible in such media. Rather, filled with engravings made from wooden blocks, *Frank Leslie's Illustrated Newspaper* was the predecessor of all illustrated weeklies in the United States, and this would eventually include *Time* and *Newsweek*.

Regardless of Leslie's ambitions, it was the Civil War of course that helped fuel the success of his newspaper, as well as that of his two major competitors, *Harper's Weekly* and the *New York Illustrated News*. Published in New York City, *Frank Leslie's Illustrated Newspaper* took a Northern view of the sectional crises, while sending its own small army of reporters and sketch artists into the heart of the Confederacy to compile as complete a record of

events as possible. From early on, as the paper's circulation climbed, Leslie never had to worry about keeping his staff in the field busy day and night. The dozens of sketches and reports that weekly made their way into the published paper in the Civil War years between 1861 and 1865 were testaments to the validity of Leslie's original vision and mission.

Today the name of Frank Leslie is in part synonymous with the Civil War itself. That association was underscored in 1895 with the publication of *Frank Leslie's Illustrated History of the Civil War*, a one-volume compilation that the publisher produced as a means of preserving "in a convenient and permanent form" the many historic sketches and the valuable firsthand commentaries that accompanied them.

In a similar endeavor, the Smithsonian, in association with HarperCollins, now presents *Witness to the Civil War: First-hand Accounts from Frank Leslie's Illustrated Newspaper*. Once again Leslie's visual drama comes alive, offering an almost encyclopedic look at the war and its many trappings. In page after page, the still-vibrant woodblock illustrations recall the grandeur of the fortifications, the animation of the battlefields, and give shape and meaning to the peculiar-looking ironclad navy vessels, the bustle of the sutler's store, the solitude of the picket's campfire, and the row upon row of hospital beds filled with the wounded.

Interspersed throughout the book, and of special interest, is a selection of color photographs of Civil War artifacts from the collections of the Smithsonian Institution. This inclusion of uniforms, weapons, flags, and spyglasses, and the accompanying annotations, lend an even greater sense of reality to Frank Leslie's remarkable illustrated record of the Civil War.★

—James G. Barber, Historian,
National Portrait Gallery

PREFACE

Federal Flag

Confederate
Honor Guard

As the years roll by, and the reverberating echoes of the great Civil War that shook our country from one end to the other slowly die away in the distance, the pictures of the stirring scenes of '61 to '65, drawn in the very midst of the strife, become not only interesting and attractive to the eye, but highly important and valuable as real, authentic representations of the way in which the events actually took place that no word description could possibly give.

To preserve in convenient and permanent form these valuable illustrations and to present to the public a grand panorama of the leading events of the war is the purpose of this book. The brave soldiers who, clad in the "Blue" or the "Gray," participated in the fierce struggles that marked the four years of war, will find here familiar scenes, and will be taken back, through the medium of excellent pictures, to the days they will never forget; those who "remained at home" will be reminded, in looking over these pages, of the exciting eagerness with which the appearance of each number of Frank Leslie's publications, with their famous war pictures, was awaited, and how every piece of news and illustration from the seat of battle was anxiously scanned; while those who were not born or were too young to remember now those stirring times will find much interest and instruction in studying the views of battles that became famous and have taken a prominent place in the nation's history.

The pictures in this work have been reproduced from the original cuts made by Frank Leslie's corps of war artists. They were taken from his publications because of their assured authenticity. They were drawn and engraved directly from sketches made on the scene of battle by the most famous artists of the time, and can therefore be relied upon as, absolutely accurate. They are really the most authentic war illustrations that have ever been published.

Swapping Lies

The short, concise history of the war is intended to give the reader, in as few words as possible, a complete and accurate account of the great conflict from beginning to end; describing, in entertaining language, the circumstances that led to the struggle, the important battles both on land and sea, the men who participated in them, and the causes that brought about the downfall of the Confederacy. This description, with the graphic illustrations, will, it is hoped, bring about a better knowledge and a more correct idea of the Civil War than any yet presented to the public.

Neither trouble nor expense has been spared to make FRANK LESLIE'S ILLUSTRATED HISTORY OF THE CIVIL WAR perfectly reliable in every way. Editors of experience have gone over the whole work carefully and verified every date, so as to prevent the possibility of error. ★

Terrible Effect Of A Discharge Of Grape From Fort Jackson On The Federal Gunboat "Iroquois," Captain De Camp, April 24th 1862, Which Killed Eight And Wounded Seven Seamen, Out Of A Dahlgren Gun's Crew Of Twenty-five Men, Under Lieutenant McNair.

One of the most terrible events of this desperate battle was the slaughter on board the gunboat Iroquois. *In the midst of the engagement of the 24th of April, 1862, a discharge of grape from Fort Jackson killed eight and wounded seven, out of a gun's crew of twenty-five men, at the same minute. A spectator of the horrible scene told our artist it was one of the most appalling things he had ever seen, but it only nerved the survivors to renewed exertions. Lieutenant McNair fought his gun with great gallantry, and was one of those who escaped.*

CHAPTER 1
A NATION IN CRISIS

Scene On Floating Battery, Charleston Harbor, During Bombardment Of Fort Sumter.

A very important factor in the bombardment of Fort Sumter was an immense floating battery, which did effective work in the silencing of the fort's guns. Major Anderson directed many of his shots at the floating battery; but while it was struck fifteen or eighteen times, not the slightest impression was made upon its iron-cased sides.

Abraham Lincoln,
16th President Of The United States.

THE UNITED STATES CIVIL WAR began on April 12, 1861, with the Confederate bombardment of Fort Sumter in the harbor of Charleston, South Carolina, but sectional animosity had been building for decades. Increasingly hostile controversy over slavery brought the free states of the North into direct confrontation with the slaveholding states of the South.

In the 1850s, Southerners demanded expansion of their so-called "peculiar domestic institution" into the territories, but antislavery advocates bitterly objected. When Congress left the issue up to the populations of the territories, violence erupted, especially in Kansas. Then, in October 1859, Kansas settler John Brown, a native of Connecticut, seized the government armory at Harpers Ferry, Virginia, and called for a slave uprising. With twenty-one men, including a dozen freed slaves, Brown battled a company of marines led by former West Point superintendent Robert E. Lee, who surrounded and captured the raiders.

Found guilty of murder and treason, Brown was hanged, but his raid further enflamed both sides of the slavery issue. Abolitionists saw him as an inspired martyr, while slavery supporters despised him as a wicked fanatic bent on sparking a bloodbath in the South. The resulting upheaval gained thousands of new adherents to the antislavery Republican Party, whose candidate, Abraham Lincoln of Illinois, won the presidency in 1860. Immediately, South Carolina seceded from the Union, and other slaveholding states followed.

On February 4, 1861, Mississippi's Jefferson Davis was elected president of the Confederate States of America. Now South Carolina demanded that Federal troops evacuate Fort Sumter. Lincoln refused, and on April 12, South Carolina began cannonading the fort. Two days later, Sumter's commander, Major Robert Anderson, surrendered and sailed with his garrison to New York.

Other states began to secede, including Virginia, which prepared to take over the lightly defended Harpers Ferry armory and its ninety thousand muskets. Learning of the impending danger, the armory commander set fire to the buildings and escaped with his little garrison. Next, Virginia troops captured the navy yard at Gosport, acquiring two thousand heavy guns and several warships—one of which, the USS *Merrimack*, would be converted into the ironclad CSS *Virginia*. ★

Fort Sumter, Charleston Harbor, South Carolina, 1861.

Fort Sumter, whose capture by the Confederate soldiers marked the real beginning of the Civil War, was built on an artificial island, immediately within the mouth of Charleston Bay, S.C. It took ten years to build, and cost half a million of dollars. The fortification was of a pentagonal form, built of solid brick masonry. The walls were fifty feet in height, and from eight to ten feet in thickness, and were pierced for three tiers of guns, besides necessary loopholes for musketry, and designed for an armament of 140 pieces of ordnance of all calibres. Castle Pinckney was a small fort on the southern extremity of Shute's Folly Island, in Charleston Harbor, S.C. Though it was not in itself formidable, its position gave it great local importance, as it commanded the whole line of the eastern wharves. It had two rows of guns, the lower being in bombproof casemates, the embrasures for which were about seven feet above low-water mark, and the upper being en barbette. The armament of the Castle consisted of about twenty-five pieces, 24- and 32-pounders, a few seacoast mortars and six columbiads.

Castle Pinckney, A Fort Defending Charleston Harbor, S. C., 1861.

General P. G. T. Beauregard.

Major Robert Anderson.

Burning Of The United States Arsenal At Harpers Ferry, Va., April 18th, 1861.

The arsenal at Harpers Ferry contained a large quantity of machinery and arms, and was garrisoned by a small detachment of United States Rifles, under the command of Lieutenant Roger Jones. Having been apprised of the approach of an over-whelming force of Confederates, under instructions from the Governor of Virginia to seize the arsenal, Lieutenant Jones, in order to prevent its falling into the hands of the enemy, set fire to the building, which was soon a mass of flames. Lieutenant Jones and his men then fled across the Potomac and reached Hagerstown about seven o'clock the next morning. The government highly commended the lieutenant for his judicious conduct, and promoted him to the rank of captain.

The Sixth Regiment of Massachusetts Militia Leaving The Jersey City Railroad Depot In Answer To Lincoln's Call To Defend Washington, D. C., April 18th, 1861.

Thousands of patriotic citizens filled every available space in the big railroad station in Jersey City when the Sixth Regiment of Massachusetts entered, on its way to defend the Capital, Washington, April 18th, 1861, after marching through the streets of New York. The people enthusiastically cheered the soldiers and wished them a safe journey as they boarded the waiting train. The regiment was composed of eight hundred men. This was the regiment which, upon its arrival in Baltimore, was stoned and shot at by a mob of Southern men who attempted to stop its progress to Washington.

TO THE DEFENSE OF WASHINGTON

The Northern states immediately answered President Lincoln's call for seventy-five thousand militia, sending troops to defend Washington, which was in danger of being occupied by Confederate forces.

On April 19 the Sixth Massachusetts Militia was the first regiment of "Nationals"—as Union, or Federal, troops were termed—to arrive at Baltimore. As the regiment marched from one railroad station to another, it was attacked by a mob of ten thousand secessionists. Assaulted with clubs, stones, and firearms, the soldiers, one thousand strong, fought back, sometimes firing into the crowd. Four militiamen and a dozen rioters were killed. The regiment was prevented from going on to Washington, because insurgents had destroyed the railroad tracks leading to the capital.

Within two days, New York's Seventh Regiment and the Eighth Massachusetts Regiment had opened communication with Washington by seizing and repairing a railroad line from Annapolis, Maryland. The first of these troops entered Washington on April 25 to cheering from Union supporters lining the streets. Thousands more soldiers soon followed and built earthworks, forts, and camps until Washington became a vast citadel.

In May, Federal troops crossed to Virginia and took possession of Alexandria. This force included the Eleventh New York Regiment, known as Fire Zouaves because they had been recruited from New York City firemen. Their colonel,

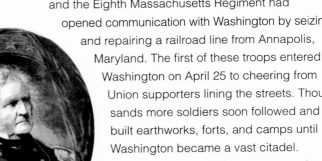

Lieutenant General Winfield Scott.

Elmer E. Ellsworth, had won fame in 1859–60 as leader of the Chicago Zouaves, a spectacular cadet drill team that toured the country. According to *Leslie's*:

> The Secessionists in Alexandria naturally did not relish the capture of their city by the Federals, and the proprietor of the Marshall House showed his resentment by refusing to take down the Confederate flag flying on his roof. Seeing this, Colonel Ellsworth, with one or two of his zouaves, rushed up the stairs and pulled down the offending colors. As they descended with the flag in their hands the tavern keeper picked up a gun and shot the gallant young colonel dead, only to be immediately killed himself by one of the zouaves.

Late in May, a Federal flotilla commanded by Captain J. H. Ward ascended the Potomac River and destroyed Virginia's heavy batteries at Acquia Creek, about sixty miles below Washington. Ward was killed, but Virginia lost control of the Potomac. ★

Commonly called a kepi, the forage cap was the most popular headgear of the Union armies. This style originated with the French Foreign Legion in the early 1850s and made its way to America just before the Civil War.

The Seventh Regiment, N. Y. S. M., Passing Down Cortland Street On Their Way To The Pennsylvania Railroad Depot, En Route For Washington, D. C., April 19th, 1861.

From the moment it became known that the pet regiment of New York, the gallant Seventh, was to be the first body of citizen soldiers to leave the city for the war, the excitement among the people was intense. Early on the morning of April 19th, 1861, there was an extraordinary excitement in the city. Windows along the whole line of march were taken possession of, and groups of people accumulated on the stoops of houses and at the corners of every street. Deafening cheers greeted the soldiers everywhere. During a temporary halt a venerable man rushed in front of the staff, and cried out: "God bless you, boys! Do your duty—fight for your flag!"

Jefferson Davis.

Murder Of Colonel Ellsworth At The Marshall House, Alexandria, Va., May 24th, 1861.

Colonel Ellsworth was passing the Marshall House in Alexandria, Va., when he saw a Confederate flag waving above it. On the spur of the moment he entered the hotel, and ascending to the roof with two or three friends, cut the halyards and took possession of the flag. As he descended the stairs he was fired at by James W. Jackson, proprietor of the hotel. Colonel Ellsworth fell to the ground mortally wounded.

Funeral Cortege, At Boston, Mass., Of Sixth Massachusetts Soldiers Killed At Baltimore.

The funeral of the four soldiers of the Sixth Massachusetts Regiment who were killed in Baltimore, April 19th, 1861, while en route to Washington, was held at Boston, May 1st. The bodies were received in the city by a military escort under Governor Andrew and Adjutant General Schouler, accompanied by a large concourse of citizens, and were temporarily deposited in the vaults of King's Chapel. The names of these "first martyrs" were Luther C. Ladd, Addison O. Whitney, Charles A. Taylor and Sumner H. Needham. The Legislature of Maryland, on March 5th, 1862, appropriated seven thousand dollars, to be dispensed, under the direction of the Governor of Massachusetts, for the relief of the families of those who were killed and injured.

Attack Upon The Batteries At The Entrance Of Acquia Creek, Potomac River, By The Vessels "Pawnee," "Yankee," "Thomas Freeborn," "Anacosta" And "Resolute," June 1st, 1861.

On May 31st Captain Ward, in command on board of the Thomas Freeborn, *and assisted by two more of his gunboats, the* Resolute *and the* Anacosta, *began the attack on the Confederate batteries,* *and after a two hour's fight, succeeded in silencing the batteries at the landing; but, for want of long-range ammunition, could not effectually respond to the heavy fire from the heights, and so had to* *withdraw. The following day, however, with additional aid from the* Pawnee *and* Yankee, *the attack was resumed, and the batteries were at last silenced and the Confederates compelled to retreat.*

THE COLORS OF WAR

A Civil War battlefield was a very confusing place. The sound of guns, the smell of smoke, distant bugle calls, Rebel yells, and undisciplined citizen-soldiers all combined to create chaos. This was particularly true at the onset of the war, when the armies of both sides were composed of rapidly organized volunteer militia units. Adding to the confusion was a dazzling array of uniforms. The lack of standard uniform colors and styles made it difficult to tell friend from foe in the heat of battle. Tunics came in shades of blue, gray, black, and green. Blue was not limited to the North; gray was not limited to the South. This often led to deadly mistakes, where friendly fire would tear into an approaching column, or conversely, fire would be withheld from an advancing enemy force.

Both sides boasted Zouave units. Their uniforms (left) were based on the uniforms worn by the elite Zouave troops of the French army. The style included a short jacket, vest, sash, baggy trousers, and a fez. While fashionable on a parade ground, the style was not practical for campaigning and was soon discontinued.

As the war progressed, both sides adopted more standardized uniforms. The Confederate uniform pictured on the right consisted of a gray frock coat with black facings and gold-colored buttons. The black belt has "CS" on the buckle. Topped with a buff slouch hat, the uniform left little question as to which side this private held allegiance.

Zouave Uniform

Confederate Uniform

General McGowen Addressing The Thirty-fifth Abbeville (S. C.) Regiment, Charleston.

The gallant band of Confederates known as the Abbeville Volunteers was composed of a hundred of the wealthiest citizens of the district. A number of them were accompanied by their Negro servants, as the barons of old were by their armed vassals. General McGowen made a strong speech, and was loudly cheered.

THE FIRST CLASHES

Early in June 1861, one of the war's first actions took place at Philippi, Virginia (later West Virginia), as General George B. McClellan of Ohio routed a Confederate force with a surprise night attack. The engagement involved a few hundred troops on each side, with minimal casualties, but this minor success began to build McClellan's reputation. Other fighting developed in eastern Virginia, where Confederates under Colonel J. B. Magruder were threatening the Union base at Fortress Monroe.

General B. F. Butler, headquartered at Fortress Monroe, took measures to oppose Magruder, sending troops led by General E. W. Pierce to rendezvous with other Union forces for an advance against Confederates at Big Bethel—or Great Bethel. These two Federal columns of mostly green troops converged in the darkness, mistook each other for enemies, and began firing. Several men were killed before the mistake was discovered. The combined columns then marched to Big Bethel, where there was a brief but sharp engagement, and Union forces were repulsed. Artilleryman Lieutenant John T. Greble was killed, becoming the first regular army officer to die

in the war. Volunteer major Theodore Winthrop of Connecticut, a member of Butler's staff, also fell at Big Bethel. This unexpected defeat greatly alarmed Northerners and heartened Southerners. The Confederacy moved its seat of government from Montgomery, Alabama, to Richmond, Virginia, where C.S.A. president Jefferson Davis made a speech "to a multitude of people," according to *Leslie's*:

He spoke some bitter words against the National Government, and after saying that there was "not one true son of the South who was not ready to shoulder his musket, to bleed, to die or to conquer in the cause of liberty here," he declared: "We have now reached the point where, arguments being exhausted, it only remains for us to stand by our weapons. When the time and occasion serve, we shall smite the smiter with manly arms, as did our fathers before us and as becomes their sons. To the enemy we leave the base acts of the assassin and incendiary. To them we leave it to insult helpless women; to us belongs vengeance upon man." ★

United States Cavalry Scouting In The Neighborhood Of Fairfax Courthouse, Va.

This picture represents a small party of Federal cavalry scouting in the vicinity of Falls Church, Va., in the late spring of 1861. Falls Church was the scene just before of a short but unfortunate skirmish in which thirty Federal troops were either captured or slain. Hundreds of soldiers, at different times, were killed by thus venturing into dangerous places of this kind.

United States Cavalry Engages The Confederates In The Neighborhood Of Fairfax Courthouse.

On June 1st, 1861, there was a smart skirmish between B Company, U.S. Dragoons, under Lieutenant Tompkins, and a body of 1,500 Confederates, at Fairfax Courthouse, Va. The Federal cavalry charged into the town, meeting with a brisk fire from houses on both sides of the street and from all quarters of the town. Lieutenant Tompkins's horse was shot under him, and falling beneath the animal, he sprained his ankle. After being completely inclosed by the Confederates for a short time Lieutenant Tompkins and his men fought their way out, taking with them seventeen prisoners.

Financing the war was a continuing problem for both North and South. As a new nation, the Confederate States of America issued its own currency, but this was rapidly deflated as more and more paper money was printed. The Confederate paper dollar was worth eighty cents (in gold) in December 1861, and had fallen to one and a half cents by war's end in April 1865.

Camp Corcoran, On Arlington Heights, Va., Near Washington. The Sixty-ninth Regiment, New York State Militia, Digging Trenches And Erecting Breastworks.

Camp Corcoran was situated just beyond Arlington House, opposite Georgetown. It was occupied by the Sixty-ninth Regiment of New York. One of the first duties of these soldiers after enlisting for the war was the digging of trenches and erecting of breastworks around this camp. They worked unremittingly and with such success that their position became of immense strength. The result of their work was pronounced by military authorities to be perfect and admirable in every respect. The camp was named Corcoran in compliment to their colonel, who was greatly respected.

Review Of The Clinch Rifles On The Parade Ground In Front Of The Arsenal, Augusta, Ga.

The parade ground of the Augusta Arsenal is one of the finest in America, being nearly a mile square. It is well laid out, and overlooks the city and surrounding country. The view is splendid. The Clinch Rifles were famous for their efficiency, and were considered one of the best companies in the State, holding the right of the battalion volunteer companies. They were named after General Clinch. They were organized in 1851 by Captain S.C. Wilson, a veteran of the Florida War.

THE CALL TO DUTY

In northern Virginia, just across the Potomac from Washington, General P. G. T. Beauregard was marshaling a growing force of Confederates. There were a few skirmishes, but the Confederate government denied it intended to assault Washington and said it would make war only if attacked. Federal leaders believed otherwise and also suspected the British government was scheming to recognize Southern independence. According to *Leslie's*:

Both inside and outside the capital plans were being made to attack it. General Beauregard . . . was preparing to march upon the city, and in the halls of Congress and in the President's house secret emissaries were supposed to be prowling about, bent upon some deadly purpose. Several of the European governments were beginning to recognize the Southern Confederacy, and were preparing to give it moral and material aid. Among these governments was Great Britain, and that country's open recognition of the independence of the Confederacy was prevented only by the high position taken by Secretary of State [William H.] Seward, who, in his instructions to the new representative at the Court of St. James, Mr. Charles Francis Adams, said: "You will in no case listen to any suggestions of compromise by this government, under foreign auspices, with its discontented citizens. If . . . you shall unhappily find her majesty's government tolerating the applications of the so-called Confederate States or wavering about it, you will not leave them to suppose for a moment that they can grant that application and remain the friends of the United States."

Not only were men on both sides enlisting as volunteers, in what *Leslie's* described as "enthusiasm at fever heat," but women also were doing their patriotic duty, organizing a medical system to care for sick and wounded troops. Miss Dorothea Dix, superintendent of Union nurses, was the best known of these volunteers. Both North and South developed soldiers' aid societies to improve the living conditions of the troops, and hospitals were set up at major railroad junctions, where wounded troops could be cared for before moving on to the next stop. ★

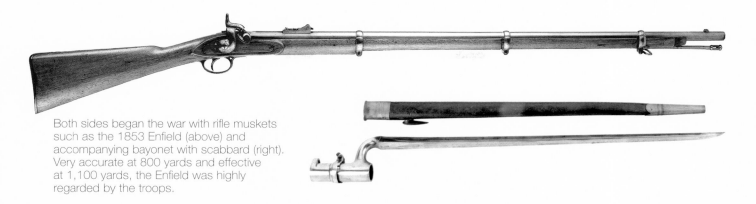

Both sides began the war with rifle muskets such as the 1853 Enfield (above) and accompanying bayonet with scabbard (right). Very accurate at 800 yards and effective at 1,100 yards, the Enfield was highly regarded by the troops.

The Fight At Philippi, Va., June 3d, 1861 — The United States Troops Under Command Of Colonel Dumont, And The Confederates Under Colonel Porterfield.

Acting under instructions from Brigadier General Morris, the Federal troops were arranged in two columns, one commanded by Colonel B. Kelley and the other by Colonel E. Dumont. It was agreed that Colonel Kelley's command should proceed along the Beverly Turnpike, above Philippi, with the view of engaging Colonel Porterfield's rear, when Colonel Dumont's column would simultaneously open fire from the heights overlooking the village. Colonel Kelley being delayed by a treacherous guide, Colonel Dumont made a dash upon the Confederate pickets, carrying consternation in their ranks and capturing the barricaded bridge across the river. Colonel Kelley then arrived and pursued the fugitives through the streets of Philippi until he was badly wounded.

Battle At Great Bethel Between The Federal Troops Under General Pierce And The Confederate Troops Under Colonel Magruder, June 10th, 1861.

The Federal troops, on arriving at Great Bethel, June 10th, 1861, found the Confederates in great force under Colonel John B. Magruder, and posted behind batteries of heavy guns. The first intimation they had of the presence of the enemy was a heavy fire. After bravely standing their ground and succeeding in slacking the enemy's fire, they were ordered to retreat by General E.W. Pierce. A number of gallant officers were killed, among them Lieutenant J.T. Greble and Major Theodore Winthrop. The Federal troops retreated in splendid order. The cause of their defeat was explained by the incompetency of General Pierce.

WAR IN THE MOUNTAINS AND ACTION AT SEA

In early July, as the main Federal and Confederate armies took up positions for the coming campaign in northern Virginia, General McClellan moved with ten thousand men against Confederate positions in the Virginia mountains. He divided his force for this operation, intending to strike several enemy positions at the same time.

Upon learning that Colonel John Pegram, with a large body of Confederates, was entrenched at Rich Mountain Gap, McClellan sent Ohio colonel W. S. Rosecrans, with a number of Ohio and Indiana soldiers and a troop of cavalry, to drive them out. Rosecrans led his force, as *Leslie's* reported, on

a circuitous and perilous route up to the top of a ridge of Rich Mountain, above Pegram's camp. Here the Confederates caught sight of them, and Pegram, with 600 men, armed with muskets and cannon, attacked them vigorously. The battle was a hot one for some time, but Rosecrans at last succeeded in driving the enemy back and taking possession

Battle Of Rich Mountain, Between A Division Of Major General McClellan's Command, Led By General Rosecrans, And The Confederate Troops Under Colonel Pegram, July 11th, 1861.

Upon the arrival of General McClellan's troops on the Beverly Pike, which runs along the summit of Rich Mountain, a heavy fire was opened upon them, the Confederates firing shot, shell and grape, but so wildly that little damage was done. The Federal troops dropped flat, and deployed as skirmishers, advancing slowly. The enemy, mistaking this movement, rushed from their breastworks with a shout and approached the road. The Federals then fired a most terrific and destructive volley, and rushed up the slope into the enemy's ranks with fixed bayonets. The fight now raged promiscuously all over the hill. The Confederates were soon driven up the hill, over their breastworks, and completely routed. The battle continued for an hour and a half from the first to the last shot.

Capture Of The Propeller "Fanny" In Pamlico Sound By Three Confederate Steamers While Conveying Men And Stores To The Twentieth Indiana Regiment.

On the 1st of October, 1861, Colonel Hawkins dispatched the propeller Fanny, *with two cannon, ammunition, supplies and provisions, to the camp of the Twentieth Indiana Regiment, then stationed at Chicamacomico. While they were landing their stores into boats they were attacked, about five o'clock in the afternoon, by the Confederate steamer* Northampton *and two tugs, which came from the direction of Roanoke Island, and after a brief engagement the* Fanny *was surrendered to the enemy.*

of its position. For his gallantry on this occasion Rosecrans was commissioned a brigadier general. Soon afterward, when McClellan was appointed to the command of the Army of the Potomac, Rosecrans succeeded him in Western Virginia.

Pegram soon regrouped his troops and was reinforced, but McClellan arrived and captured him and six hundred men. Another force was defeated at Carrick's Ford by McClellan's troops as the region was temporarily cleared of Confederate soldiers.

By now, the Confederates had organized a fledgling naval force of twenty armed vessels, fitted out to attack United States merchant commerce. The first, *Lady Davis*, was named in honor of the C.S.A. president's wife. Another, the *Petrel*, made a fatal error in mistaking the United States Navy frigate *St. Lawrence* for a merchantman. As the *Petrel* made its way toward the frigate, well-aimed cannon fire abruptly sent the Confederate vessel to the bottom.

Meanwhile, Union forces began to advance on Richmond, and the Confederates prepared to meet them. In the western theater—the Missouri and Mississippi valleys—thousands of volunteers were maneuvering for their first engagements. ★

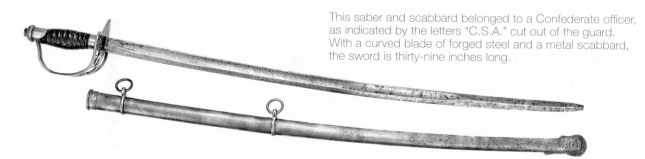

This saber and scabbard belonged to a Confederate officer, as indicated by the letters "C.S.A." cut out of the guard. With a curved blade of forged steel and a metal scabbard, the sword is thirty-nine inches long.

Battle Of Carrick's Ford, Between The Troops Of General McClellan's Command, Under General T. A. Morris, And The Confederates Under General Garnett, July 13th, 1861.

After a long march through drenching rain, the Federal troops under General Morris reached Carrick's Ford, where they found the Confederates holding the cliff on the opposite bank of the river.

Both sides began a heavy firing. Then the Seventh Indiana Regiment plunged into the river and scaled the cliff on the right of the enemy, while the others kept up the fight in front. As soon as the flanking

party reached the top of the cliff the Confederates retreated, and were pursued for about two miles. Confederate commander R.S. Garnett was killed, the first general of the war to die in action.

OLD GLORY AND THE STARS AND BARS

First Confederate National Flag

U.S. National 34-Star Flag

C.S.A. Battle Flag

The most famous symbol of the Confederacy was never officially adopted as its national flag. The Confederate battle flag (left), sometimes called "The Southern Cross," was designed by General P. G. T. Beauregard following the First Battle of Bull Run (First Manassas). On the battlefield it had been difficult to distinguish the First National Flag of the Confederacy (upper right) from "Old Glory" (bottom right). Beauregard wanted a banner easily identifiable through the smoke of battle. The Confederacy's first national flag, known as the Stars and Bars, was adopted in one of the first acts of the Confederate Congress. This flag was raised over the Capitol of the Confederate States of America in Montgomery, Alabama, on March 4, 1861. On this same day, President Abraham Lincoln was taking the oath of office on the steps of the Capitol in Washington, D.C. "Old Glory" entered the war with thirty-four stars, one for each state (including those that had seceded from the Union). Two more stars, for West Virginia and Nevada, had been added to the Union flag that flew over Appomattox at war's end.

The Railroad Battery Protecting The Philadelphia, Wilmington, And Baltimore And Ohio Railroad.

This remarkable railroad battery was built of half-inch boiler iron, and was proof against the best rifles at any distance. The sides had fifty rifle holes, *and at one end was a 24-pounder cannon, which moved on a pivot, with a gun carriage complete. The Federal railroad battery accommodated sixty men. The* *car itself was built to assist workmen in rebuilding the bridges between Havre de Grace and Baltimore. At night it was used as a berth and guard car for the men.*

Ellsworth's Chicago Zouave Cadets.

No military organization during the war was more brilliant than the Chicago Zouave Cadets, with their striking and gay uniforms; their flowing red pants; their jaunty crimson caps; their peculiar drab gaiters and leggings, and the loose blue jackets, with rows of small, sparkling buttons, and the light-blue shirt beneath. In all their evolutions the Zouaves displayed great precision.

CHAPTER 2
NORTH AND SOUTH AT WAR

The Battle Of Bull Run, Between The Federal Army, Commanded By Major General McDowell, And The Confederate Army, Under Generals Johnston And Beauregard, On July 21st, 1861.

The first battle of Bull Run was fought on July 21st, 1861. It resulted in a loss on the Federal side of 481 killed, 1,011 wounded and 1,460 missing. The Confederate loss was estimated at nearly 2,000. The latter army, in action and reserve, numbered over 40,000 men, while the Federal force in action was about 35,000. Although the Confederates won a great victory, they were in no condition to pursue the advantage they had gained; had they done so they might have converted a repulse into a disastrous and total defeat. Our illustration shows the Federal troops advancing on the enemy's lines.

Passage Down The Ohio River Of General Negley's Pennsylvania Brigade (77th, 78th And 79th Regiments, Pennsylvania Volunteers).

One of the most striking and interesting scenes during the war was the passage down the Ohio River of General Negley's brigade, consisting of the following regiments, all of Pennsylvania; Seventy-seventh, under Colonel Hambright; Seventy-eighth, Colonel Stambrough; Seventy-ninth, Colonel Sewall. These regiments were dispatched in six river steamers for the purpose of re-enforcing the Federal army in Kentucky, as there was then great probability of the Confederate troops making that State a camping ground during the winter, if not driven out by the Federals.

ON JULY 16, 1861, General Irvin McDowell advanced in several columns with fifty thousand troops—mostly three-month volunteers—against Beauregard's Confederates at Manassas Junction and along Bull Run. McDowell intended by a series of feints to surprise the enemy in their rear and drive them from Manassas. Neither side thought the other would stand and fight.

The Federal columns met with little opposition as the Confederates withdrew, following Beauregard's prearranged plan to lead McDowell into a dangerous position. The Federals advanced in high spirits, thinking they were driving the enemy before them, but they were brought to a stop at Blackburn's Ford, on Bull Run, by troops under General James Longstreet. Repulsed, the Union force withdrew to Centreville, where McDowell regrouped and waited a few days for supplies.

At two o'clock on the morning of July 21, the Federal army moved to attack the Confederate left, which had been strongly reinforced by the arrival on railroad cars of General Joseph E. Johnston's troops from the Shenandoah Valley. By now, thousands of civilian spectators had come out from Washington in carriages and on horseback to watch the struggle from a distance.

The Confederates slightly outnumbered McDowell, and the battle was closely fought, with attack and counterattack. Virginia general Thomas J. Jackson earned the nickname "Stonewall" for firmly holding his position as fighting raged in the summer heat. The slaughter was unexpectedly terrible, but it began to seem the Federal troops were winning. Then fresh Confederate reinforcements suddenly arrived and turned the tide. McDowell's troops broke, and their retreat became a rout, soldiers mingling with terrified civilians, all fleeing for their lives.

After the battle, according to *Leslie's*, "A great exultant shout arose throughout the South… while a deep gloom settled upon the North." For both sides Bull Run was sobering as they counted their losses and realized the enemy was determined to fight. The Federals suffered at least twenty-six hundred casualties, the Confederates almost two thousand.

Away in the western theater, more bloody battles were on the horizon, and the exploits of generals Halleck, Grant, Pope, Lyon, Price, Van Dorn, and Polk would be followed in every American town and village. ★

Battle Of Bull Run, Va., July 21st, 1861, Between The Federal Army, Commanded By General McDowell, And The Confederate Army, Commanded By Generals Beauregard And Johnston.

The battle of Bull Run, which the Confederates called the battle of Manassas, was the first really important action of the Civil War. The scene lay a few miles northwest of Manassas Junction, on the banks of Bull Run. It resulted, as everyone knows, in the complete routing of the Federals. The repeated efforts to rally the troops were fruitless. In a short time the entire Federal line seemed to have broken in disorder, the force under General Sykes apparently alone making an effort to withstand the tide. But it was finally compelled to yield to the masses against it. The Federals then on all sides retreated in confusion toward the passages leading to Centreville. By nine o'clock that evening the last of the fugitives had reached Centreville. The Confederate loss was reported to be 378 killed, 1,489 wounded and 20 missing —total 1,887; that of the Federals, 481 killed, 1,011 wounded and 1,460 missing —total 2,952.

Reception By The People Of New York Of The Sixty-ninth Regiment, N. Y. S. M., On Their Return From The Seat Of War, Escorted By The New York Seventh Regiment.

The return home of the gallant Sixty-ninth Regiment—composed entirely of Irish citizens—on Saturday, July 27th, 1861, was an ovation as warm and enthusiastic as their endurance and bravery deserved.

Their service of three months had been of infinite value to their country and honor to themselves and their State. The Sixty-ninth had rendered good service at Arlington Heights, and especially distinguished itself

at the battle of Bull Run. On the morning of their arrival the streets were crowded with people, and the gallant fellows were greeted with shouts of applause along the whole line of march.

WAR IN MISSOURI

Military developments in the Missouri region favored the Union in the summer of 1861. General Nathaniel Lyon had taken control of St. Louis, St. Joseph, Hannibal, and key Mississippi River points. Confederate guns at Memphis, Tennessee, however, blocked river navigation.

In early August, Lyon learned that Confederate general Sterling Price, encamped in southwestern Missouri, had been strongly reinforced. Rather than allow Price to take the initiative Lyon went on the offensive. Though he had fewer than six thousand troops to face almost twelve thousand, Lyon compelled the Confederates to retreat to Wilson's Creek, where he pursued them, and the decisive contest began:

The battle opened furiously. In the thickest of the fight was Lyon. Wherever needed he would dash in and give encouragement to his men by words and deeds. Although his horse was shot under him, and he was wounded in the head and leg, he was soon on another horse, and, placing himself at the head of the . . . troops, he swung his hat over his head, and dashed forward with a determination to gain a victory. But a bullet in his heart stopped him, and he fell back dead.

After two more hours, the combatants broke off the fight, and the Union withdrew. There were approximately twelve hundred casualties on both sides.

The Charge Of The First Iowa Regiment, Under General Lyon At The Battle Of Wilson's Creek, Which Was Fought Near Springfield, Mo., August 10th, 1861.

The battle of Wilson's Creek, Mo., was fought August 10th, 1861. It was a bloody conflict, one of the most fiercely contested of the war, and resulted in a Confederate victory. The First Iowa Regiment especially distinguished itself. Under the leadership of General Lyon the men made a gallant charge upon superior numbers. Although wounded in the head and leg and his horse killed, General Lyon quickly mounted another horse and dashed to the front of his regiment. He was among the first to be killed. The battle-weary Federal forces withdrew, and Price's forces occupied Springfield.

Now the Union high command's strategy was to defeat Price, seize Little Rock, Arkansas, and put into service a flotilla of gunboats being built near St. Louis. These boats would break through at Memphis and continue advancing southward, ultimately to attack New Orleans. The Confederates, however, held the advantage, and early in September Price compelled the surrender of Lexington, Missouri, and three thousand troops.

New Union operations developed in November, as General Ulysses S. Grant moved against the garrison at Columbus, Kentucky, commanded by General Leonidas Polk. Grant captured a strongpoint at Belmont, Missouri, across the Mississippi from Columbus, but Polk counterattacked. Four thousand Confederates engaged Grant's three thousand, and the Union troops had to fight their way to safety. Each side lost more than six hundred men. ★

Communication between military units was a major difficulty. The Confederacy established a Signal Corps early in 1862, making it the first independent branch of service for military signalmen in history. This spyglass was used to read messages signaled by flags or flashed torches and lights.

Death Of General Nathaniel Lyon, At The Battle Of Wilson's Creek, Near Springfield, Mo.

The fiery General Lyon fell at the head of his outnumbered army in a desperate fight at Wilson's Creek, Mo., on the 10th of *August, 1861, while leading a charge against the Confederate forces under the Texan, General Ben McCulloch. General* *Lyon was educated at the U.S. Military Academy at West Point, where he was graduated with distinction in 1841.*

First Charge Of Frémont's Bodyguard, Led By Major Zagonyi, On The Confederate Garrison Defending Their Encampment At Springfield, Mo., October 25th, 1861.

While encamped at Pomme de Terre, Mo., Frémont learned that a Confederate force had just been established at Springfield. He at once ordered Major Zagonyi to take his cavalry on a reconnaissance, and to capture the camp if deemed practicable. When Zagonyi arrived near Springfield he learned that the Confederate force was nearly 2,000 strong, while he had but 150 men. Notwithstanding this disparity he made a gallant charge into the enemy's ranks in the face of a hailstorm of bullets. He succeeded in forcing the Confederates to break away in wild disorder, thus making the first charge of the bodyguard a great success.

The Trent Affair

The Civil War had only just begun when President Abraham Lincoln almost found himself in another war, this one with Great Britain, over the "Trent Affair."

On November 8, 1861, the USS *San Jacinto*, commanded by Captain Charles Wilkes, stopped the British mail steamer *Trent* in international waters off the coast of Cuba. On board were James Mason and John Slidell, official representatives of the Confederacy to Great Britain and France. Acting without authorization, Wilkes had the two removed under the threat of force and taken to Fort Warren in Boston Harbor, triggering a diplomatic crisis. Wilkes was celebrated as a hero and the House of Representatives voted him a special gold medal.

The incident was, however, viewed quite differently on the other side of the Atlantic. An outraged Lord Palmerston, the British prime minister, demanded the immediate release of the two diplomats. Queen Victoria's government was ready to declare war, and went so far as to move eight thousand troops to Canada in preparation of an invasion.

Cooler heads prevailed. Prince Albert, consort of Victoria, was on his deathbed when he insisted the strong language of the official communication to Washington be toned down. Secretary of State William Seward sent a carefully worded response. While the United States did not apologize, it did release the Confederates.

Henceforth, President Lincoln's policy of "one war at a time" was strictly followed.

Sword was presented by the City of Boston to Charles Wilkes, USN.

Battle Of Belmont, Mo., November 7th, 1861 — Federal Forces Commanded By U. S. Grant; Confederate Forces, By Leonidas Polk.

Brigadier General Grant and staff direct the movements of the troops as Brigadier General McClernand leads the charge at the head of the Thirty-first Illinois. Across the Mississippi River is Columbus.

Embarking Troops And Artillery At Bird's Point, Mo., By Order Of General Frémont.

The threatening attitude which General Hardee, who commanded the Confederates near Cape Girardeau, on the Mississippi, assumed after the battle of Wilson's Creek, toward Ironton, the terminus of the St. Louis and Iron Mountain Railroad, rendered some movement necessary. General Frémont, having no force to spare from St. Louis, in consequence of the singular apathy of the Minister of War, consequently ordered four regiments and a sufficient force of artillery from Bird's Point.

UNION VICTORIES

The hostilities in the Virginia mountains seemed to end in the summer of 1861, but they were renewed in the autumn. General Robert E. Lee, in charge of Confederate forces there, was ordered to drive Federal troops across the Ohio River and defeat the army under General W. S. Rosecrans. Success would open the way for a Confederate invasion into Maryland, Pennsylvania, and Ohio.

These plans failed when Rosecrans refused to wait for an enemy attack and instead brought on a battle with General John B. Floyd, at Carnifex Ferry. Floyd escaped under cover of darkness, and soon afterward Lee's force also was defeated and had to join him. Union successes soon put an end to the war in this part of Virginia. Lee had failed in his first campaign in the field, but he soon would be called to Richmond as military adviser to President Davis.

In important coastal action late that summer, a Union naval expedition with approximately nine hundred troops commanded by General B. F. Butler captured two Confederate forts at the entrance to Hatteras Inlet, on the North Carolina coast. In October another expedition commanded by Admiral S. F. du Pont, with fifteen thousand troops under General Thomas W. Sherman, sailed for

Port Royal Sound, near Hilton Head. A severe tempest off Cape Hatteras wrecked four transports, but the rest of the expedition gathered at Port Royal Sound.

The entrance to this sound was guarded by two Confederate batteries, while within the sound was a small flotilla of armed vessels commanded by Commodore [Josiah] Tatnall, late of the United States Navy, who had espoused the Confederate cause. On the morning of November 7th Du Pont silenced the two forts and drove Tatnall's fleet into shallow water. The National troops then took possession of Port Royal and the neighboring islands. At the close of 1861 the National authority was supreme over the coast islands from Warsaw Sound to the mouth of the North Edisto River.

With these and other successful amphibious operations, the Union blockade of the Southern coast was well under way.★

The Model 1861 was the most common rifle musket on the battlefield during the war. It fired a .58 minié ball and was moderately accurate up to a hundred yards. Nearly one million were manufactured for the Union infantry.

Night Attack On The Federal Forces Under Major Bowen, Occupying Salem, Mo., By The Confederate Forces Under Colonel Freeman, December 8th, 1861.

Sneaking upon an enemy at night is a very good policy if you succeed in catching him while he still sleeps; but if he should wake up in time he is generally in the maddest and most ferocious humor, and doubly dangerous. Colonel Freeman found this to be the fact. Company B pitched into his men like savages, slashing right and left, and pouring volleys of pistol and carbine shots into the crowd which blocked up the street and filled the yards around the houses in a thick, confused mass. Their superior numbers were only an impediment, and when another company, which was in an adjoining stable, broke loose upon them, and Company A commenced to get out of the house, while Company D, having mounted its horses, came clattering down the street with a wild whoop, they had to seek safety.

The Bombardment Of Fort Walker, Port Royal Harbor, S. C. — View Of The Interior During The Bombardment By The Vessels Of The Federal Fleet, November 7th, 1861.

Fort Walker was an irregular bastioned and curtained work, constructed on a bluff eight feet above high-water mark, and in a position commanding important points and channels in Port Royal harbor. The whole plan of attack had been admirably arranged by Commodore du Pont, *and was at once daring, simple and original. It was for the ships to describe a circle following one another, each giving its fire on the fort as it steamed past. The firing on both sides was incessant, and about noon the* Wabash, Bienville *and* Susquehanna *approached within six hundred yards of the fort, and delivered their broadsides with a deliberation and effect which was terrible. This desperate combat lasted for three hours, principally with 10-second and 5-second shells, when the firing ceased, the guns in the fort being completely silenced.*

Destruction Of Guns And Gun Carriages At The Arsenal, Beaufort, S. C., By Captain Ammon Of The United States Gunboat "Seneca."

On November 14th, 1861, a party commanded by Captain Ammon landed at Beaufort, S.C., from the United Sates gunboat Seneca, visited the arsenal and destroyed the cannon they found there. Having burnt the gun carriages and knocked off the trunnions, they considered their work complete.

Rescue Of Major Reynolds's Battalion Of Marines From The Foundering Steamer "Governor."

While being used as a transport, off Cape Hatteras, November 2d, 1861, the steamer Governor, *Commander Phillips, foundered in the rough sea. Those on board, a battalion of marines under Major Reynolds, were transferred with great difficulty to the* Sabine. *The* Governor *was a sidewheel steamer of 650 tons burden. She was built in New York city in 1846, and was originally intended for river navigation.*

Explosion Of A Shell In The Cutter Of The U. S. Steamer "Niagara," November 3d, 1861.

Few incidents in the war displayed more courage and coolness than the action of Fog Boatswain A.W. Pomeroy, of the United States frigate Niagara, *in burning the Confederate brig* Nonsuch *near New Orleans. After setting the vessel on fire the Federal sailors were pulling back to the* Niagara, *when a shell struck the boat, throwing two of the officers in the water. The men were saved by a cutter dispatched from the* Niagara.

Scene In The Military Market At Beaufort, S. C.

Union soldiers buy food and wares at a market in Federal-occupied South Carolina, bargaining with mainly African-American merchants and traders.

Morning Mustering Of The "Contrabands" At Fortress Monroe, Going To Their Day's Work.

As a living illustration of one of the aspects of the Civil War, a sketch is given below of the contrabands—escaped slaves—going to their daily work at Fortress Monroe.

George B. McClellan (1826–85) was a brilliant administrator and strategist but an over-cautious field commander. Lincoln accused him of having a case of the "slows," and at one point asked if he could borrow the army since the general was not using it.

McClellan's nonregulation uniform coat (left) was worn at the Battle of Antietam.

This custom-made chess set was used by McClellan during his service.

Grand Review In Washington Of Eight Batteries Of Artillery And Three Regiments Of Cavalry By President Lincoln, General McClellan And A Portion Of The Cabinet, September 24th, 1861.

General McClellan held a grand review of cavalry and artillery, which went off with great éclat. The troops consisted of two full regiments of cavalry—the Fifth Regulars and the Kentucky Volunteers—together with such portions of the Lincoln, Ira Harris and Cameron Guards as had their horses and sabres. These made up above two thousand men, and in addition there were eight batteries of United States regular flying artillery, comprising forty-eight heavy rifled and howitzer field pieces, with caissons, carriages, horses, riders and runners in full quota. The review was held on a broad, level common one mile east of the Capitol, at about 3 P.M.

McCLELLAN REBUILDS THE FEDERAL ARMY

On July 27, 1861, General George B. McClellan assumed command of the Federal army in and around Washington and named it the Army of the Potomac. A West Point engineer and former railroad executive, McClellan set high standards for training, equipping, and supplying his troops, and spirits soon lifted among the rank and file.

He at once became so popular in this position that when, a few months afterward (November 1st) General [Winfield] Scott resigned his place as general in chief of the armies, on account of old age and ill health, McClellan was appointed to that office. He immediately set to work to reorganize the army, which had been shattered by the terrible blow at Bull Run.

The Northern and Southern armies in the East remained in a standoff. Then, in October, the Union cause was again shaken by another defeat—minor, but demoralizing—when a small expedition was ambushed and repulsed at Ball's Bluff, Virginia. The Union commander, former Oregon senator E. D. Baker, a good friend of President Lincoln's, was killed in the action, which cost 921 Union casualties but only 149 Confederate.

Union operations on western waters—the Mississippi, Ohio, Cumberland, and Tennessee rivers—were progressing under the leadership of General H. W. Halleck. Although Confederates were building strongholds, the Union had the advantage of their armored gunboat fleet, soon to undertake important duties. ★

Death Of Colonel Baker At The Battle Of Ball's Bluff, Va., October 21st, 1861.

Colonel E. D. Baker, while commanding the First California Volunteers, which formed part of General Stone's brigade at the battle of Ball's Bluff, and who had just before he entered the battle been notified of his appointment as brigadier general, was killed while at the head of his command, pierced by bullets in the head, body, arm and side. He died as a soldier would wish to die, amid the shock of battle, by voice and example animating his men to brave deeds.

Battle Of Roanoke Island, February 8th, 1862 — Decisive Bayonet Charge Of The Ninth New York Volunteers (Hawkins's Zouaves), On The Three-gun Battery Manned By The Confederates.

Our illustration was taken at the moment when the enemy, not waiting to receive the bayonet charge of the Zouaves, who were then in the very act of springing over the parapets, fled in utter confusion, throwing away their arms and accoutrements to facilitate their escape. It was at this important moment that the Fifty-first New York Regiment, Colonel Ferrero, who had advanced on the battery by a flank movement on the left, planted the Stars and Stripes in triumph over the ramparts.

ATTACKING THE CONFEDERACY FROM THE EAST AND WEST

In January 1862 attention again turned to coastal operations as a hundred warships and transports, commanded by Commodore L. M. Goldsborough and carrying sixteen thousand soldiers under General A. E. Burnside, left Hampton Roads for Roanoke Island and Pamlico Sound on the North Carolina coast. Roanoke Island was strongly fortified with Confederate batteries that had to be destroyed.

An attack was made upon these fortifications the first week in February. Goldsborough took a fleet of seventy vessels into Croatan Sound and

Death Of General Zollicoffer, In The Battle Of Mill Springs, Ky., January 19th, 1862.

While the Confederate waves were surging against the Federal breakers the opposed were several times carried so close to each other that portions of each were mixed up with the other, and hand-to-hand encounters were not unfrequent. Owing to the consequent confusion, the commanders of both sides at times unknowingly came in dangerous vicinity to foes. At one time two mounted officers came trotting along the right flank of the Fourth Kentucky, and noticing their firing upon Confederates near by, shouted to them, "Don't fire on your friends; they are Mississippians." Colonel Fry at this juncture came up the front of his regiment, and with a glance recognized in one of the officers General Zollicoffer. In a twinkling he had pulled out his revolver and fired at the Confederate chieftain, putting a bullet through his breast and causing his fall from the horse and instant death. The Confederate aide put spurs to his horse, and quickly spread the news among the Confederates of the fall of their general.

opened on the batteries. These shots received a hearty response from the batteries and from a flotilla of small gunboats. The bombardment lasted all afternoon, and at midnight about 11,000 New England, New York and New Jersey troops were landed on the island led by General J. G. Foster. [Enemy] redoubts, one after the other, were captured, although the Confederates, far inferior in number, made a gallant defense. A particularly brave stand was made in the last redoubt, but through a furious charge by Hawkins's Zouaves they were compelled to beat a retreat and submit to capture after a short flight.

Confederate (top) and Federal (bottom) belt plates.

thousand Union troops under General S. R. Curtis were encamped in the vicinity of Pea Ridge in the Ozark Mountains, when Confederate general Earl Van Dorn attacked with seventeen thousand men. The battle continued for two days, ending in a resounding Confederate defeat. On January 19, Confederates led by General F. K. Zollicoffer were defeated in Kentucky near Mill Springs, and their commander was killed. These setbacks spurred the Confederacy to send Beauregard to take charge of operations in the region.

In early February, a Union expedition was mounted to open an invasion route southward along the Tennessee and Cumberland rivers. Twelve gunboats under the command of Commodore A. H. Foote and fifteen thousand troops led by General Grant first attacked Fort Henry on the Tennessee River. After heavy bombardment, the fort surrendered, and nearby Fort Heiman also was captured. ★

Meanwhile, the Missouri theater was extremely active, with sixty battles and skirmishes fought from June 1861 to late February 1862. On March 7, eleven

General Asboth And Staff At The Battle Of Pea Ridge, Ark., March 6th–8th, 1862.

The gallantry displayed by General A.S. Asboth in the victory of Pea Ridge gives great interest to the spirited sketch of himself and staff which we present to our readers. Among the officers in the sketch were Acting Brigadier General Albert, Brigade Quartermaster McKay, the young commander of the Frémont Hussars, Major George E. Waring, Jr., from New York city, formerly major of the Garibaldi Guards, and the general's aides-de-camp, Gillen and Kroll, etc. Among General Asboth's most constant attendants was his favorite dog, York, a splendid specimen of the St. Bernard species.

CHAPTER 3
'ON TO RICHMOND'

Bombardment Of Fort Henry — Interior View — Bursting Of A Rifled 42-pounder Gun, February 6, 1862.

The fleet of gunboats commanded by Commodore Foote steamed up the channel, and reached the head of the island soon after 12 o'clock. At 12:34 the Cincinnati opened with an 80-pounder shell which screamed over the water, dropped squarely into the fort, and produced a great commotion among the Confederates. The boats kept steadily on, slowly but constantly in motion, and the fire was kept up deliberately and with regularity. The shots, some of them, went beyond the fort into the camp, and smashed the barracks about, making kindling wood of the log huts, and sending terror and dismay to the soldiers. The artillerists in the fort stuck well to their guns, and fired with great coolness and accuracy of aim, many of their shots striking the boats. They lost the use of their rifled 42-pounder, it bursting on the fourth fire. Still onward moved the boats—straight on—their bows puffing out immense volumes of white smoke and sending their missiles into the fort. Soon one of the Confederate guns was dismantled, and then fire from the fort perceptibly slackened. The fleet kept steadily on, pouring in their shells slowly but surely. The shells tore through the embankment, knocked the gabions and sandbags about, and smothered the garrison with sand. One shell burst directly over one of the guns, and killed or wounded every Confederate at it. Commodore Foote was still getting nearer and nearer, and was about three hundred yards distant when the Confederate flag came down.

The United States Transport "Terry" Pushing Her Way Through The Swamps And Bayous, Back Of Island No. 10, To The Assistance Of General Pope At New Madrid.

The task of forcing vessels through the bayous to General Pope, at New Madrid, proved one of unusual difficulties. The United States transport Terry, *in advance, drawing less water than any other, succeeded in forcing her way through to New Madrid, and opened a passage for steamers to General Pope's command below Island No. 10.*

AFTER CAPTURING FORT HENRY, Grant moved against Fort Donelson, on the Cumberland River in Tennessee. Donelson was commanded by former secretary of war John B. Floyd, considered by Unionists to be a traitor who had conspired to keep the United States military weak prior to the outbreak of hostilities. On February 14 Grant's troops and Commodore Foote's gunboats attacked Donelson, but the gunboats received a tremendous pounding from shore batteries and had to withdraw.

The Confederates counterattacked Grant but were defeated and driven back. It soon became apparent to Floyd that the fort would have to surrender. Fearing the charge of treason if captured, he fled under cover of night.

The next morning, Grant's reply to Donelson's request for surrender terms became famous: "No terms other than unconditional and immediate surrender can be accepted." His initials, "U. S.," were said to mean "unconditional surrender"—which did follow on February 16. As many as eight thousand Confederates were captured.

The Confederates now evacuated garrisons in several cities, and Nashville, too, fell into Federal hands. Next, General John Pope drove the Confederates from New Madrid and advanced on Island No. 10, a Mississippi River strongpoint commanded by General Beauregard. On March 16 the guns and mortars of Foote's gunboats opened upon the fortified island, and a siege began. In an effort to bypass the island, Union troops cut a canal across a flooded peninsula for gunboats to pass through, but the falling river allowed the passage only of lighter transports.

Finally, a Union ironclad braved a tremendous cannonading from the shore batteries and forced a passage in the main river channel during a thunderstorm. As this daring feat was accomplished, the vessel was greeted with wild hurrahs from Pope's troops. Days later, another ironclad got through. Then, under cover of these gunboats, Union regiments crossed the river, threatening to cut off all retreat from the fort. Unwilling to be taken, Beauregard left Island No. 10 to a subordinate and departed with a number of his best soldiers. Island No. 10 fell the next day, April 8, with more than thirty-five hundred men, a great blow to the Confederacy, and producing widespread alarm in the Southern states. ★

Bombardment Of Island No. 10 And The Fortifications Opposite On The Kentucky Shore, By The Federal Mortar Boats And Gunboats, March 17th, 1862.

Capture of Fort Donelson — Charge Of The Eighth Missouri Regiment And The Eleventh Indiana Zouaves, Commanded By General Wallace, February 15th, 1862.

General Lew Wallace, whose troops were comparatively fresh, made the assault. Cruft's brigade, headed by the Eighth Missouri and the Eleventh Indiana, from Colonel Smith's division, with two Ohio regiments in reserve, formed the assailing column. Across the valley, or extended ravine, in Wallace's front, was a ridge which had been yielded. Up this ridge a charge was made. Before them lay an ascent of one hundred and fifty yards; and a lively bushwhacking followed between them and the Confederate pickets. When less than fifty yards had been gained they received a volley from the hilltop. Smith ordered his men to lie down; and when the heavy firing was exhausted they arose and pushed on up the hill, at last reaching the top. The fight and pursuit lasted for nearly two hours, and by five o'clock the enemy had entirely disappeared from the field.

Colonel Lewis Wallace, Of The Eleventh Indiana Volunteers (Zouave Regiment), And His Staff, On Service In Western Virginia.

This gallant officer, pictured with members of his staff, was the commander of the Eleventh Indiana Volunteers. He first distinguished himself in Western Virginia. His regiment rendered good service, against all the efforts of the enemy, in a difficult and dangerous country.

COUNTERATTACK AT SHILOH CHURCH

In early April 1862 Grant's army of forty-two thousand men was encamped at Pittsburg Landing, on the left bank of the Tennessee River, near Shiloh Church. He was preparing to move against Corinth, Mississippi, which controlled railroad communications between the Mississippi and the East. Grant was not expecting an enemy attack, but forty thousand Confederates had secretly come up from Corinth to assemble within a few miles of Shiloh Church. This force was under General Albert S. Johnston, seconded by Beauregard.

On the morning of April 6 the Union camp awoke to the crash of musketry and warning shouts from pickets, as the first assault struck General William T. Sherman's troops near the church. Although taken by surprise, the half-dressed Union troops rallied and held as long as possible, then withdrew to rally again. For ten hours the battle raged, and by nightfall the Federals had been

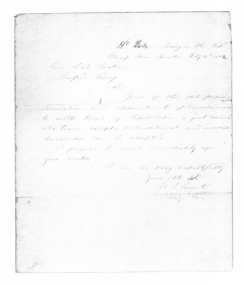

"No terms other than unconditional surrender can be accepted," wrote Ulysses S. Grant in this February 16, 1862, letter to his Confederation counterpart, General Simon Bolivar Buckner, demanding the surrender of Fort Donelson. It was the first major Union victory of the war and earned Grant the nickname "Unconditional Surrender Grant."

pushed back to the Tennessee River. General Johnston, however, had been killed.

During the night Grant was reinforced by twenty thousand troops under General D. C. Buell. When the fight resumed, the outnumbered Confederates under Beauregard expected reinforcement by General Van Dorn from Arkansas. When word came that Van Dorn could not get across the Mississippi in time, Beauregard ordered a withdrawal. The exhausted Federals did not pursue. The Confederates lost more than ten thousand men, the Federals thirteen thousand. *Leslie's* writers were guilty of wishful thinking when they said:

> Beauregard's army . . . fell back to Corinth, and Grant would have pursued it, and, in its weak condition, probably captured it, had not General Halleck, his superior at that time, come up just then from St. Louis, and ordered the troops to rest for awhile. This gave the Confederates a chance to reorganize their forces and make themselves ready for another battle.

Halleck's command grew to one hundred and ten thousand men, while Beauregard could raise only sixty-six thousand. Within weeks, Union troops triumphantly entered abandoned Corinth without a fight. On June 6 Foote's gunboats defeated the Confederate squadron defending Memphis, which also was then evacuated. ★

Battle Of Shiloh, Or Pittsburg Landing — Left Wing — The Woods On Fire During The Engagement Of Sunday, April 6th, 1862 — Forty-fourth Indiana Volunteers Engaged.

The right wing of General Hurlbut's division stopped the advance of the Confederates by a determined defense along a side road leading through the woods on the right of the field. The Twenty-fifth and Seventeenth Kentucky and Forty-fourth and Thirty-first Indiana Regiments were engaged. By some means the dry leaves and thick underbrush which covered this locality took fire, filling the woods with volumes of smoke, and only discovering the position of the opposing forces to each other by the unceasing rattle of musketry and the whizzing of the bullets.

Battle Of Shiloh, Or Pittsburg Landing — Colonel Johnson Endeavoring To Capture A Confederate Officer, But Gets Only A Wig.

Colonel A.K. Johnson of the Twenty-eighth Illinois Regiment has, during the late war, shared in the dangers of many a daring adventure. On the last day of the action at Shiloh, or Pittsburg Landing, and while the Confederates were flying in confusion from their works, three of the officers in their flight passed very near the place where Colonel Johnson was stationed. The colonel instantly started in pursuit. Coming within pistol range, he fired at the nearest of his flying foes. This brought the Confederate officer down on his horse's neck. Colonel Johnson, believing this to be a feint to avoid a second shot, determined to drag him from his saddle by main force. Riding up to his side for this purpose, he seized him by the hair of his head, but to his astonishment and disgust he only brought off the Confederate major's wig. Instantly recovering his headway, he again started for the delinquent, but his pistol had done its work, and before the colonel reached him his lifeless body had fallen from the saddle.

Burnside Expedition — The Fleet And Transports Off Hatteras During The Storm — The General Giving Orders To His Officers.

Never had any expedition in the history of the world to pass through a severer ordeal; everything seemed to conspire against it—nature with her storms, and human nature with her villainy. In addition to the warring elements there was the subtle treachery of Northern traitors who deliberately periled the lives of thousands for the sake of gain. Compared to such men as the New York contractors whom gallant Burnside anathematized in the bitterness of his heart even Judas Iscariot becomes human. Our correspondent wrote that one of the most exciting scenes during this trying crisis was when, off Hatteras, General Burnside sprang up the rigging of the vessel to give his directions.

CAMPAIGNS ON THE SOUTHERN COAST

In March 1862 General A. E. Burnside and fifteen thousand troops captured New Berne, North Carolina, and Federal forces proceeded to take other important places on the coast. By April they were besieging Fort Pulaski, defending Savannah, Georgia, the home port to fast blockade runners and privateers.

For two days the fort was well defended. Then the balls and shells had played such havoc with its walls that the garrison was obliged to surrender. The gain of this important position made it possible for the Federals to close the port of Savannah against the numerous blockade runners that were then making mischief all along the coast.

Meanwhile, successful operations by Federal naval and land forces compelled the Confederates to abandon forts along the coasts of Florida and Georgia. In Florida, Jacksonville and St. Augustine were taken, and Pensacola and all nearby coastal fortifications were evacuated.

In April a seaborne force of fourteen thousand troops under General B. F. Butler arrived at the islands off New Orleans to rendezvous with Admiral David Farragut's naval squadron and a fleet of bomb vessels commanded by Commodore David D. Porter. Butler was the supreme political general, as *Leslie's* describes:

The Bombardment Of Fort Pulaski — Second Day, Friday, April 11th, 1862.

General Quincy A. Gillmore took personal command of Tybee Island on the 20th of February, 1862, and at once began the construction of earthworks. On the 9th of April everything was in readiness for the bombardment, and early on the following morning a summons for the surrender of Fort Pulaski was sent, through Lieutenant J. H. Wilson, to its commander, Colonel Charles H. Olmstead, by General David Hunter. The

surrender having been refused, order was given to immediately open fire. This was done about eight o'clock in the morning of the 10th, from the two 13-inch mortars in charge of Captain Sanford. The remaining two batteries joined in, and their united fire thundered all day, and was steadily responded to from the fort. The bombardment of the fort was kept up until the next morning, and at daybreak of the 11th the firing again

commenced on both sides. The Federal fire was mainly directed against the southeastern portion of the fort, and by two o'clock in the afternoon the breach had become so wide that the arches of the casemate were laid bare. This was followed by the hoisting of a white flag, when firing ceased. The immediate and unconditional surrender of the fort was agreed on.

Just before leaving Washington General Butler [had] said to the President: "Good-by. We shall take New Orleans or you will never see me again."

The river passage up to New Orleans was guarded at a bend in the Mississippi by forts Jackson and St. Philip. On April 18 Federal warships attempted to bombard the forts into silence. After several days of severe but inconclusive cannonading, Farragut decided to run warships by the forts and strike at New Orleans, which had few other defenses. On the night of April 23, his flagship *Hartford* led the attack on Fort Jackson, while gunboats fired at Fort St. Philip. The vessels passed the forts, and Butler advanced overland to accept their surrender as Farragut sailed up to New Orleans. He sent emissaries ashore, threatened a bombardment, and forced capitulation.

A major Confederate city had fallen, and the Mississippi was blockaded. ★

Landing Of Captain Bailey And Lieutenant Perkins On The Levee, New Orleans, With A Flag Of Truce, To Demand The Surrender Of The City To The Federal Government.

Captain Bailey, bearing a flag of truce, put off in a boat, accompanied by Lieutenant George H. Perkins, with a demand for the surrender of the city, as well as for the immediate substitution of the Federal for the Confederate ensign. They stepped ashore and made their way to the City Hall through a motley crowd, which kept cheering for the South and Jefferson Davis, and uttering groans and hisses for President Lincoln and the "Yankee" fleet. General Lovell returned an unqualified refusal, besides advising Mayor Monroe of New Orleans not to surrender the city.

The Great Naval Battle On The Mississippi — First Day's Bombardment — Federal Schooners Off Forts Jackson And St. Philip, Commanding The Passage Of The River.

The Federal offensive force consisted of six sloops of war, sixteen gunboats and twenty-one mortar vessels. These were accompanied by a large number of store-ships, tenders, etc. On the 18th of April they anchored three miles below Forts Jackson and St. Philip, and prepared for active operations. Captain Porter, commanding the mortar flotilla, wishing to ascertain their range before his actual attack, stationed the Arietta, John Griffiths and Orvetta about two and a half miles from the forts. The Arietta fired the first shot, to which Fort Jackson replied. The Confederate shots fell short more than fifty yards every time, while the effect of our shells on the fort was such that after two explosions the enemy retired from their barbette guns, and afterward only used those in casemates.

Review Of The Confederate Troops On Their March To Virginia, In Front Of The Pulaski Monument, Monument Square, Savannah, Ga., August 7th, 1861.

The Pulaski Monument is situated in Johnson or Monument Square. It is a fine Doric obelisk of marble, 53 feet in height. The base of the pedestal is 10 feet 4 inches by 6 feet 8 inches, and its elevation is about 12 feet. The corner stone was laid by Lafayette during his visit to the United States in 1825. The needle which surmounts the pedestal is 37 feet high. Another and very elegant structure has also been erected to the memory of this gallant foreigner in Chippewa Square. Pulaski was killed in the attack made by the allied American and French armies in 1779, when the British held Savannah.

Confederate soldiers are not as closely associated with the kepi as are Union infantry, but this kepi, worn by a Texas soldier, was Confederate-issue, made of gray wool with a black leather visor. Kepis were not popular with Southern troops because they did not protect the wearer from the sun or rain.

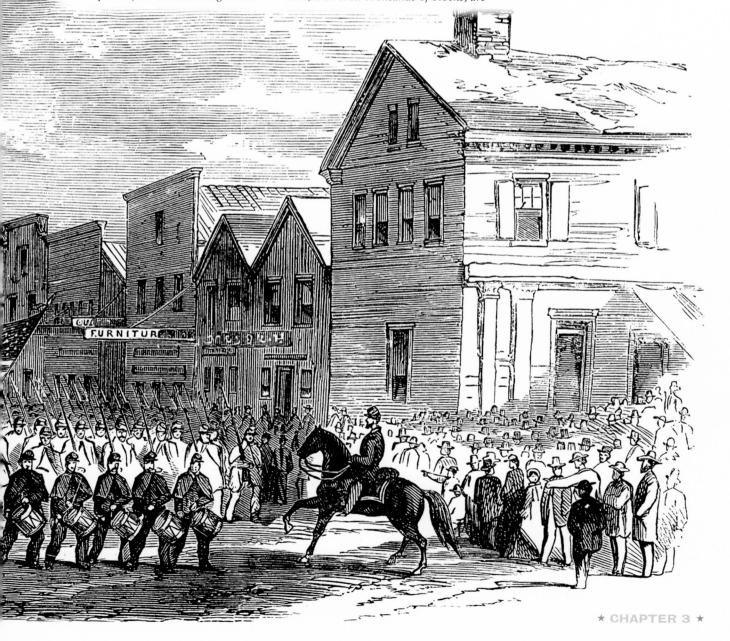

Federal Troops Marching Through Second Street, New Fernandina, Fla.

Our sketch of New Fernandina in 1862 shows the principal business street in the city, called Second Street. There seemed to be quite a joke in numbering streets *where there were not half a dozen in the place; but the spirit of imitation was strong, and as Philadelphia and New York, with their thousands of blocks, are* *simplified and rendered more easily findable by the aid of arithmetic, so must be the villages of the South.*

THE FIRST BATTLE OF THE IRONCLADS

In early 1862 McClellan's two hundred thousand–man Army of the Potomac camped near Washington, while the public demanded that something be done to crush the Confederacy. McClellan's reluctance to go on the offensive persuaded Lincoln to relieve him as general in chief.

At last, McClellan proposed to move on Richmond by way of Fortress Monroe and the peninsula between the York and James rivers. The navy began to ship troops and supplies for the campaign as many Northerners cheered "On to Richmond!"

In March a battle between two small but powerful vessels occurred in Hampton Roads, Virginia, where the Federal invasion fleet was operating. The Confederates had converted the USS *Merrimack*, one of the ships abandoned at Norfolk, into an ironclad gunboat renamed the CSS *Virginia*. On March 8 this vessel attacked Federal warships at the mouth of the James River, easily defeating the sailing frigates *Congress*, which sank, and *Cumberland*, which was forced aground. It was feared other vessels would share this fate, because the Union naval commanders could devise no means to prevent the impending disaster. But relief came to them unexpectedly that night in the shape of the *Monitor*, a small but strong gunboat, with its deck almost level with the surface of the water, and having in its centre a round tower of heavy iron. This tower was made to revolve so that its two heavy guns within could be brought to bear upon any point without changing the position of the vessel. This little craft had been constructed . . . at New York, and arrived at Hampton Roads just in the nick of time to show its usefulness.

Early the next morning the *Virginia* and *Monitor* engaged furiously, firing point-blank and wreathed with smoke, but cannonballs simply bounced off their sides, and explosive shells had little effect—even though at times the vessels actually touched. No such naval battle had ever been seen before. After three hours, both vessels withdrew. The Federal fleet was saved, and the *Virginia*, at Norfolk, was in danger of capture by the Union invasion. ★

Battle In Hampton Roads Between The Confederate Ironclad Steamers "Merrimac," "Yorktown," And "Jamestown," And The Federal Wooden Sailing Frigates, "Cumberland," And "Congress" — Sinking Of The "Cumberland" By A Blow From The "Merrimac," Saturday, March 8th, 1862.

Second Naval Battle In Hampton Roads — Fight Between The Federal Ironclad "Monitor," Of Two Guns And The Confederate Iron-plated Steamers "Merrimac," "Yorktown," And "Jamestown," Carrying Twenty-four Guns — The "Merrimac" Crippled, The Frigate "Minnesota."

Loss Of The "Monitor" — A Gallant Attempt Of The Officers And Crew Of The United States Steamer "Rhode Island," To Rescue The Crew Of The "Monitor," Off Cape Hatteras.

The closing day of 1862 will always be a dark one in our history, for just on the threshold of its birth the pet monster of our ironclads went down off Hatteras, *with our flag flying on its tower, and in the midst of a furious storm. Its sudden and unlooked-for fate recalled to every mind that memorable Sunday in March* *when it signalized its advent to war by driving back to its Norfolk retreat the terrible Merrimac.*

GUNBOATS AND IRONCLADS

After the widely reported battle between the *Monitor* and *Virginia*—*Merrimac*—in Hampton Roads, navies around the world began experimenting with designs for armored vessels. In the tumult of the Civil War, however, North and South were obliged to experiment in the fire of battle. Both sides hastened to build armored vessels, and the work-horse was the shallow-draft, screw-propelled ironclad gunboat that plied rivers and coastal waterways. The North's prodigious manufacturing capacity produced sixty *Monitor*-class vessels, which were invaluable in many campaigns. The less-industrialized South produced no new ironclads, and instead reinforced existing vessels and sheathed them with iron plate and rails. The most powerful ironclads, *Arkansas* and *Tennessee,* were soon defeated.

THE *VIRGINIA*

This scale model of the CSS *Virginia* reveals how much of the vessel was underwater—particularly its lethal bow ram, which drove a wooden Union frigate ashore on the day before the March 9, 1862, battle with the USS *Monitor* at Hampton Roads. When

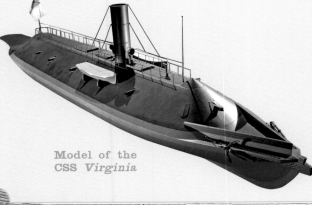

Model of the
CSS *Virginia*

Confederate forces took control of the abandoned U.S. Navy yard at Norfolk in April 1861 they found the charred and sunken hull of the USS *Merrimack*, a steam-powered frigate that the Federal government did not want the Confederacy to capture intact. Confederate engineers and shipwrights ingeniously designed and built a heavily timbered upper works on the hull and sheathed the vessel in iron plating. Although difficult to maneuver in action, this "ironclad," renamed CSS *Virginia*, was almost impregnable to the naval guns of the day. Its sloping sides caused cannon balls to bounce off, and the ram could fatally hole any wooden vessel it went up against. Northerners traditionally referred to the ironclad as the *Merrimac*, without the final *k*. The model, made of wood with plastic parts, is 68.5 inches long.

THE *MONITOR*

In September 1861, Union leaders knew the CSS *Virginia* was well under way to becoming an ironclad ram that could wreak havoc with the Federal fleet. This was when Swedish-born marine engineer John Ericsson submitted a design to the Navy Department for a completely new iron-plated gunboat. Ericsson was at first turned down with the insult:

Model of the USS *Monitor*

"It is the image of nothing in the heavens above, or the earth beneath, or the waters under the earth." Which was true. Others saw the future in his design, however, and Ericsson was contracted to build his "cheese box on a raft" for the U.S. Navy. It was built swiftly, for the *Virginia*—looking like a floating barn roof, 263 feet long—would be launched at Norfolk by spring. The USS *Monitor*, termed "Ericsson's Folly" by the press, was only 172 feet long but was more heavily armed than the *Virginia*, with eleven-inch-caliber Dahlgren guns, and was more maneuverable.

The *Monitor*'s nine-foot-high revolving turret had eight layers of inch-thick iron plate and her sides had more than four inches of iron armor. In 2002, the *Monitor*'s turret was raised from the waters off Cape Hatteras. The model is 43 inches long.

Federal Gunboats And Mortar Boats Attack Island No. 10 Between Columbus And New Madrid — Bombardment On Sunday, March 16th, 1862 — View Looking Down The River.

Arrival Of General McClellan, April 5th, 1862, To Take Personal Command Of The Federal Army In Its Advance On Yorktown — Enthusiastic Reception By The Troops.

On the 11th of March, 1862, the President issued an order relieving General McClellan of part of the responsibility heretofore devolving upon him. The order stated that "General McClellan, having personally taken the field at the head of the Army of the Potomac, until otherwise ordered, he is relieved from the command of the other military departments, he retaining command of the Department of the Potomac." Our illustration represents his arrival, and enthusiastic reception by the troops.

THE VALLEY AND THE PENINSULA

Virginia's Shenandoah Valley was a strategic avenue for an invasion of the North. Attempting to control this region, which was also a valuable source of food, Union general James Shields battled Stonewall Jackson at Winchester and Kernstown late in March. Shields was badly wounded, but the Confederates were defeated and retreated up the valley.

Early in April the Army of the Potomac, with one hundred and twenty thousand troops, began its Peninsular campaign. Facing fortifications at Yorktown held by seventeen thousand men, McClellan vastly overestimated the enemy's numbers and decided to conduct a regular siege, allowing the Confederates time to bring in reinforcements.

In May General Joseph Johnston took command of the sixty-thousand-strong Confederate force on the peninsula and withdrew toward stronger positions before Richmond. Johnston's rear guard was attacked on May 5 by Federal forces attempting to disrupt his movements, but McClellan came on the field and would not allow further pursuit.

McClellan had moved only thirty-six miles toward Richmond during the month after his arrival at Fortress Monroe. The principal reason given for this slow progress was his fear that he had not troops enough to defeat the enemy. [McClellan] kept hesitating and complaining of a want of men, although the President urged him to act at once before the enemy should gather in greater strength on his front.

In early May Union forces under General John E. Wool captured the naval base at Norfolk, abandoned without resistance. Before leaving Norfolk the Confederates set fire to the ironclad *Virginia,* which would never fight again.

Hostilities increased in Virginia's mountains on May 8 as Jackson attacked General J. C. Frémont's troops at McDowell. After a severe battle of five hours, the Union forces were repulsed and retreated. Jackson reported the next morning: "Yesterday God gave us the victory at McDowell."

Jackson now went on the offensive, beginning his monthlong Shenandoah Valley campaign, which would become famous in the annals of military history. He outfought and outmarched much larger Union forces, diverting them from supporting McClellan's attack on Richmond. ★

Reconnaissance By Colonel Max Weber's Turner Rifles In The Vicinity Of Newmarket Bridge.

Camp Of The Ninth Massachusetts Regiment In The Woods, One Mile From The Confederate Fortifications, Yorktown, Va., April 10th, 1862.

Thomas J. Jackson.

THE UNION ARMY STANDS AT RICHMOND'S DOOR

By the middle of May McClellan was within nine miles of Richmond. On May 23 and 24 sharp battles drove the Confederates back, and Federals took possession of the Richmond side of the Chickahominy River.

The proximity of the Federals alarmed the Confederate Government at Richmond, and preparations were made for a hasty flight into South Carolina if necessary. They even covered the railroad bridge leading out of the city with plank, so as to facilitate the flight of artillery, and held a train of cars in constant readiness for Davis and his Cabinet. These preparations called forth from the Virginia Legislature resolutions demanding the defense of Richmond at all hazards, and assuring the President "that whatever destruction or loss of property of the State or individual shall thereby result will be cheerfully submitted to."

McClellan continued to be hesitant, however, and did not yet launch a decisive attack.

In the Shenandoah, Jackson defeated Union troops under N. P. Banks and overran the little garrison at Front

Royal. Banks retreated to Winchester but on May 24 was attacked again and routed, abandoning a mountain of commissary stores. Other Federal columns attempted to trap Jackson and his subordinate, General R. S. Ewell. A seven-mile-long train of booty-filled wagons slowed Confederate movements, but they managed to elude pursuing Union forces. Frémont overtook Ewell at Cross Keys on June 7, but the battle was indecisive. Ewell joined Jackson at Port Republic, where they defeated a small force under Shields on June 8–9.

Before Richmond, at the end of May, Johnston launched a counterattack. Longstreet led the Confederate advance, driving back Federal troops near Seven Pines. Next, the Federals retreated to Fair Oaks Station, where both sides were reinforced, and the battle raged until nightfall. The next morning, June 1, the engagement continued for several hours, until the Confederates broke off their offensive. The battles cost five thousand Federal and more than six thousand Confederate casualties, including General Johnston, who was wounded and had to leave the field. The new Confederate commander was Robert E. Lee. ★

Advance Of The Army Of The Potomac — Occupation Of Winchester, Va., And The Abandoned Confederate Fortifications, By A Detachment Of General Banks's Division Of The Federal Army, Consisting Of The Brigades Of Generals Hamilton And Williams, March 12th, 1862.

Army Of General Frémont On Its March Up The Shenandoah Valley — Wounded And Ragged Soldiers.

Frémont crossed the mountains with as little delay as was practicable, and through heavy roads reached Strasburg just after Jackson had passed through it. There he was joined the following morning by General Bayard, who brought with him the vanguard of Shields's cavalry, and, without waiting either for re-enforcements or to afford the fatigued troops their much-needed rest, they immediately started pursuit of Jackson. They shortly after overtook his rear, with which they had a slight skirmish, and followed close upon the retreating force, until their advance was checked by the burning of the Mount Jackson bridge.

Joseph E. Johnston.

Battle Of Williamsburg, Va., On The Peninsula Between York And James Rivers, May 6th, 1862.

General Hancock's sudden charge decided the battle, for it left the real key of the position in Federal hands. With the re-enforcements which McClellan had caused to be sent him immediately upon reaching the scene, late in the afternoon, Hancock took possession of all the ground he had previously occupied, and night closed upon what proved to be a dearly bought victory for the Federals. They had, in fact, gained it after sustaining a loss of 2,228 in killed and wounded, the Confederate loss being only about half that number. Early on the 6th of May Williamsburg was occupied by the Federals, while Johnston's army was again beyond the Chickahominy.

Fort Built Around The Officers' Quarters Of The First Minnesota Regiment, Near Fair Oaks, Va.

The First Minnesota Regiment, Colonel A. Sully, little dreaming how soon they would have to abandon their handiwork to the enemy, erected a fort around the commodious farmhouse, near Fair Oaks, which, after the battle of Seven Pines May 31st, 1862, had been given to their captains and lieutenants for their quarters. The appearance was so strange that an officer of General McClellan's staff made a sketch and sent it to us.

CHAPTER 4
LEE IN COMMAND

The Burnside Expedition — Melancholy Deaths Of Passengers And Crew Members Of The Federal Vessel "Anne E. Thompson," Lost Near Cape Hatteras Inlet In January 1862.

White House Landing, Pamunkey River, Va., The Grand Depot Of The Commissariat And Ordnance Department Of The Federal Army Moving Toward Richmond.

White House Landing, on the Pamunkey River, was the grand depot of General McClellan's army, and from it there was a constant communication with Fortress Monroe and Washington. It derived its name from the house in the centre of the sketch, the residence of Mrs. Custis before she became the wife of George Washington.

Robert E. Lee.

FOR NEARLY A MONTH after the battle of Fair Oaks most of the Army of the Potomac remained south of the Chickahominy River and did not move forward despite Lincoln's desire for an all-out attack on Richmond. Meanwhile Lee had been joined by Jackson and Ewell from the Shenandoah Valley, and with this added strength he prepared to destroy the isolated Federal wing north of the Chickahominy.

While Lee's preparations for a coming offensive were under way, fifteen hundred Confederate cavalrymen under General J. E. B. Stuart set off to scout the Federal positions. The impetuous Stuart rode all around McClellan's army, burned Federal supply wagons and two schooners on the Pamunkey River, and captured and carried away prisoners, mules, and horses. Stuart's raid set an example for similar mounted exploits during the war, but it also alerted McClellan that Lee was about to strike.

McClellan set about changing his supply base from White House on the Pamunkey River—the site of the Custis family "White House" homestead in which George Washington passed the first months of married life with the former Martha Custis. McClellan also began to move troops forward for his long-awaited advance on Richmond.

On June 25, the first of the Seven Days' Battles began with a skirmish at Oak Grove, where several thousand troops on each side collided in a daylong, inconclusive battle that closed with the Confederates evacuating their positions. On the next day, the action turned to Mechanicsville, as Lee sent Longstreet and Jackson with sixty-six thousand men to defeat Fitz-John Porter's thirty thousand Union troops north of the Chickahominy. A Confederate force of twenty-five thousand, under General J. B. Magruder, launched a diversionary attack against McClellan's sixty thousand troops south of the river. The Confederates also hoped to cut McClellan's communication with his White House base.

In Lee's operation against Porter, the initial clash at Mechanicsville cost the Confederates more than thirteen hundred casualties, four times the Union losses. McClellan put the withdrawal from White House into full speed, and Union forces pulled back for the next battle, at Gaines's Mill. ★

Looking Southeast From The Vicinity Of Mechanicsville, Scene Of The Battles Between Federal Forces Commanded By General McClellan And The Confederate Armies Led By General Lee.

About 2 o'clock in the afternoon, June 26th, 1862, the Confederates were seen advancing in large force across the Chickahominy, near the railroad, close to Mechanicsville. Placing their batteries in the rear of the Federals, the Confederates commenced a steady fire. The Federal batteries replied, and very soon the roar of artillery was deafening. For three hours the fight raged with great fierceness, the enemy attempting a flanking movement, which was defeated.

Battle Of Charles City Road — Charge Of The Jersey Brigade — The First New Jersey Brigade, Rushing To Support General Kearney's Division, Thus Turning The Fortunes Of The Day, June 30th, 1862.

Burning Of White House — Federal Troops, By Command Of General McClellan, Abandoning Their Position And Breaking Up The Commissariat Depot On The Pamunkey River, June 26th, 1862.

The Confederate raid of Stuart's cavalry at Garlick's Landing and Tunstall's Station had struck the occupants of the White House Landing with a deep sense of insecurity; and, consequently, when they received orders on Wednesday, June 25th, to prepare for the hasty removal of all government stores, they set to work with great activity, and by Thursday the greater portion of the heavy stores were embarked on board the numerous transports lying in the river. Unfortunately, through some accident the White House took fire, and the house of Washington's wife was soon destroyed.

LEE PURSUES McCLELLAN'S WITHDRAWAL

Porter's corps was ordered to cover the army in its withdrawal to the James River. Porter was attacked near Gaines's Mill by Generals Longstreet and A. P. Hill and so hard-pressed that McClellan ordered out reinforcements to support him.

Early on June 28 the Federal army proceeded to move its supply depot, much of it by boat, the rest overland.

In the procession was a train of 5,000 wagons, laden with ammunition, stores and baggage, and a drove of 2,500 head of beef cattle. General Lee did not learn of this movement, so skillfully was it masked, until the army was far on its way toward a new position on the James River. He then determined to overtake and destroy, if possible, the retiring army.

McClellan's rear guard fought off an attack at Savage's Station and fell back to White Oak Swamp, where they were again attacked as Lee tried to capture the supply train, which had passed just a few hours earlier. ★

George B. McClellan.

View Of The Federal Army's Formations During The Battle Of Gaines's Mill, Friday, June 27th, 1862.

At eleven o'clock each division, brigade, regiment and gun was in place. Some were in the broad, open field and others under the cover of the woods. The day was intensely warm, and many of the men, worn out with their previous day's fighting, lack of sleep and toilsome march, had already thrown themselves upon the ground and were indulging in a short slumber, when a sharp volley and then the roar of artillery announced that the Confederates had opened the fight. The Federal batteries, after some little delay, replied, and for an hour this artillery duel and shelling the woods continued. It was not till near three o'clock in the afternoon that the engagement became general, and then the battle raged for four hours with unexampled fury. Federal reinforcements counterattacked, and finally the Confederates rolled back like a retreating wave. This was the close of the day's fight.

Battle At Willis Church, Monday, June 30th, 1862 — Federal Forces, Under General Heintzelman.

This desperate battle was fought at Willis Church, a place midway between the White Oak Swamp Bridge and Turkey Bend. Our sketch represents the position of part of the Federal army at ten o'clock in the morning, just as the battle was commencing. The baggage train is in the foreground, and the enemy is advancing upon the Federal lines. Willis Church is on the left of the illustration, being what most of the Southern places of worship were, mere wooden barns.

Battle Of White Oak Swamp Bridge, Monday, June 30th, 1862 — Federal Artillery Firing.

After the battle of Savage's Station the Federals continued on their retreat. After crossing White Oak Creek the Federals had quickly formed a new line of battle at Willis Church, General Hancock's forces being on the extreme right, while *Porter's occupied the left, and Heintzelman's and Sumner's the intervening space. Jackson's advance was checked by the destruction of the bridge, and when he reached the creek, at about noon, he found the approaches well defended by* *artillery. Jackson opened upon Hancock's troops, and made repeated efforts to rebuild the bridge under cover of his heavy artillery, but he was every time repulsed.*

President Lincoln, Attended By General McClellan And Staff, Reviewing The Federal Army, On Tuesday, July 8th, 1862, Near Harrison's Landing, Va.

Confederate Forces Under Jackson Advancing Upon The Rappahannock Station, August 23d, 1862, The Commencement Of The Battles Between Pope And Lee, Ending At Bull Run, August 30th.

Reception Of Wounded Soldiers By The Federal Authorities At Fortress Monroe, Va. — The Cars Conveying Them To The Hospital; Surgeons Dressing Their Wounds.

One of the most terrible features of war is the fact that the proportion of those who die by agonizing inches is four times greater than those who fall in battle. Our sketch speaks for itself; it is a truthful picture of the solemn cost of the gigantic effort to save the Union. When the poor fellows—some Confederates and some Federals—arrived at the wharf they were landed with as much tenderness as possible, and when the weather admitted, their wounds were examined and dressed. Then they were placed in the long cars and taken to the hospital.

RETURN TO BULL RUN

Lincoln appointed Henry Halleck general in chief, and General John Pope took command of the newly formed Union Army of Virginia. Both men had seen success in the western theater, but the arrogant Pope was not well accepted by other field commanders. Frémont refused to serve under him and was replaced by General Franz Sigel, also from the West.

On August 9, Jackson defeated part of Sigel's force at Cedar Mountain, Virginia, and threatened Pope's right flank. A daring cavalry raid by General Fitzhugh Lee captured Pope's headquarters—the commander was away—and discovered that reinforcements from McClellan's Army of the Potomac would soon arrive to increase Pope's force to one hundred and thirty thousand. Lee had only fifty-five thousand men, but he moved to destroy Pope before reinforcements came.

Jackson, with twenty-four thousand men, confused and worried Pope by marching around him and destroying the Federal supply depot at Manassas Junction. Pope marshaled all his forces against Jackson, but meanwhile Longstreet was bringing up thirty thousand Confederate troops to join in the battle. On August 28 Pope led seventy-five thousand troops against Jackson, first clashing at Groveton, which cost each side about seven thousand men. Pope renewed the battle the next morning, not expecting Longstreet soon would arrive to support Jackson. Repeated Union assaults were repulsed, and on August 30, Longstreet counterattacked.

The Confederates skillfully drew [Pope] into an ambuscade on a part of the former battle ground of Bull Run . . . and a most sanguinary conflict was the result. The Federals were badly defeated and were sent flying across Bull Run to Centreville.

Pope withdrew into Washington's defenses and soon was ordered back to the West. The Army of Virginia became part of the Army of the Potomac under McClellan, who maneuvered to keep between Lee and the capital. The Second Bull Run campaign inflicted sixteen thousand Union and nine thousand Confederate casualties. ★

Manassas Junction, Showing The Evacuated Confederate Fortifications, Abandoned Camps And Wagons, And The Ruins Of The Railway Depot And Other Buildings Burnt By The Confederates.

The sight here cannot be portrayed. The large machine shops, the station houses, the commissary and quartermaster store houses, all in ashes. On the track stood the wreck of a locomotive, and not far down the remains of four freight cars *which had been burned; to the right 500 barrels of flour had been stored and 300 barrels of vinegar and molasses had been allowed to try experiments in chemical combinations; some 50 barrels of pork and beef had been scattered around in* *the mud, and a few hundred yards down the track a dense cloud of smoke was arising from the remains of a factory which had been used for rendering tallow and boiling bones.*

Forging Ironwork For Gun Carriages At The Watervliet Arsenal, West Troy, N. Y.

A more thorough and comprehensive establishment cannot be found. It embraces the whole scope of manufacture which properly belongs to an arsenal. The various departments are superintended by competent foremen, the whole governed by a commandant, assisted by ordnance officers. Watervliet is on the Hudson River near Albany, N.Y.

RICHMOND MUSKET

Confederate troops carried various types of firearms, and many were issued the model 1855 rifle musket manufactured with machinery taken from the U.S. Armory at Harpers Ferry. This 1855 model shoulder arm was made in the Richmond Armory—a model also manufactured at North Carolina's Fayetteville Armory. The rifle musket was a term adopted in 1855 for shoulder arms that maintained the form of muskets but had "rifled" rather than smooth barrels. "Rifling" means cutting spiral grooves inside the barrel, which imparts a spin to the bullet and makes it extremely accurate. The Richmond rifle musket fired a .577 caliber bullet and had a shorter barrel than a musket, which facilitated the use of a sword-type bayonet. Richmond produced approximately half the total ordnance issued to C.S.A. forces, including 323,231 infantry arms. The armory also manufactured 1,647 artillery pieces, 34,067 cavalry carbines, 6,074 pistols, 72.5 million rounds of small-arms ammunition, and 921,441 rounds of artillery ammunition.

Richmond Musket

The Ordnance Armory, Charleston, S. C. — The Volunteer Troops Trying The Arms.

The Confederate Ordnance Armory at Charleston, S.C., contained a splendid collection of arms, among which were specimens of all the arms known in modern warfare. Here were found the Minie, Warner and Colt's rifles, muskets of every possible make—breech, muzzle and chamber-loading pieces; also the terrible ten- and twelve-shooters known as Lindsay's repeaters. With this latter death-dealing weapon all the officers in the company were armed.

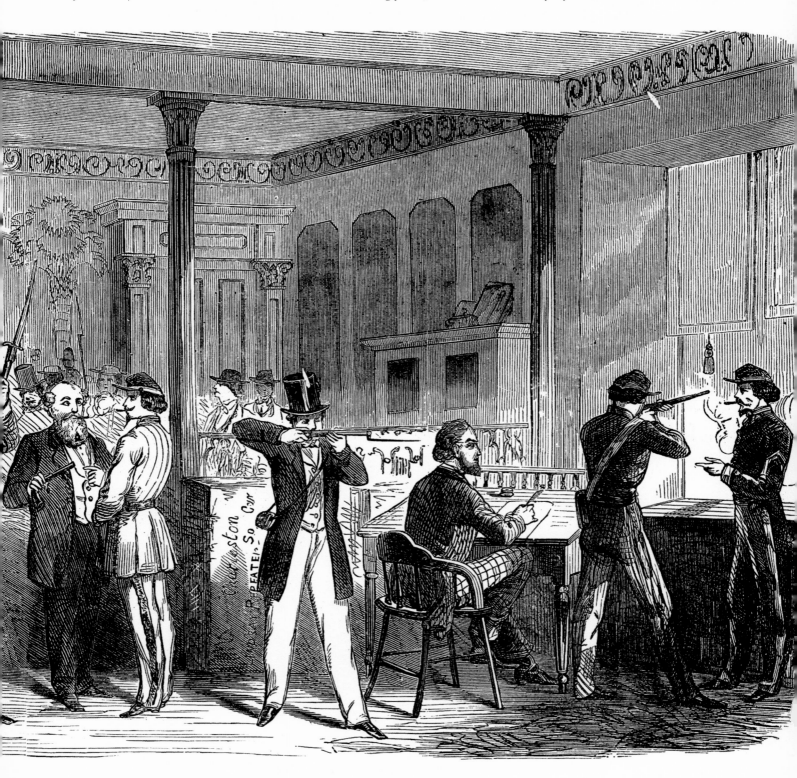

Federal Artillery Taking Up Position At The Battle Of South Mountain.

The Federal movement was admirably executed in the face of the well-directed fire from the Confederates, who had the advantage of position and could contest almost every inch of the steep, wooded and rocky approach. By four o'clock (September 14th, 1862) the engagement became general, and the entire ground was vigorously contested until the crest was reached and darkness put an end to the fight. In this engagement the total loss on both sides in killed, wounded and missing was 4,500. Union general Jesse L. Reno and Confederate general Samuel Garland Jr. were killed.

DRUMS AND DRUMMERS

Both armies employed field drummers to sound various calls and signals to troops in camp, on the march, and in the field. The loud rat-a-tat-tat of this Union snare drum, often accompanied by the shrill of a fife, could be heard above the din of battle, sending signals from commanders to their men. In camp, field drummers—usually boys of sixteen or younger—sounded calls to parade and meals, and to work details such as fetching wood and water. This military-issue, wooden-bodied snare drum, manufactured in Philadelphia, was carried by a private in the Twenty-second New Jersey Volunteers.

Union Drum

Battle Of Antietam — The Centre And Right Wing Of McClellan's Army, Engaged With The Confederate Army Led By General Lee, Wednesday, September 17th, 1862.

Stuart's Confederate Cavalry, After A Raid Into Pennsylvania, Escaping With Their Stolen Horses Into Virginia By Crossing The Potomac, Sunday, October 12th, 1862.

FROM ANTIETAM TO FREDERICKSBURG

Lincoln called for three hundred thousand volunteers in the summer of 1862, and Confederate leaders knew they must win a crushing battle to compel the North to make peace. Lee advanced into Frederick, Maryland, enticing McClellan to pursue him.

When Lee's army entered Frederick all Union flags were ordered to be hauled down. This order was obeyed by everyone except a patriotic old woman named Barbara Frietchie, and the national ensign was flying from her window when Stonewall Jackson . . . approached. Jackson ordered his riflemen to shoot away the staff. As the flag fell the woman snatched it up and waved it defiantly. Admiring her pluck, Jackson's nobler nature, as [John Greenleaf] Whittier says,

within him stirred
To life at that woman's deed and word:

"Who touches a hair of yon gray head
Dies like a dog! March on!" he said.

In mid-September McClellan's forces engaged Confederates screening Lee's advance to Antietam Creek, near Sharpsburg, Maryland. Meanwhile, the Harpers Ferry garrison surrendered to Jackson, who hurried to join Lee. McClellan had seventy-five thousand troops, and Lee more than forty thousand.

On September 17 General Joseph Hooker opened the Battle of Antietam with an attack from the Union right wing. On the Union left, General A. E. Burnside forced the crossing of a key bridge, and the battle raged as the bloodiest single day of the war. The contest became a standoff, however, with 12,410 Federal casualties and 10,700 Confederate.

Lee withdrew during the night of September 18, and Lincoln ordered pursuit, but McClellan was reluctant. In early November, Lincoln relieved him of command, and Burnside took his place.

By early December, Burnside's 106,000 Federals faced Lee's 72,500 Confederates across the Rappahannock River at the Battle of Fredericksburg. On the evening of December 12 the Federal army crossed the river on pontoon bridges, and the battle began the next morning. Burnside's repeated suicidal assaults on Lee's entrenched line were bloodily repulsed, with 12,700 casualties, while the Confederates lost 5,300.

Burnside withdrew, defeated, on December 15. ★

Burnside Assuming Command Of The Army Of The Potomac — Issuing Orders To His Staff.

"November 10th, 1862.—In accordance with General Orders, No. 182, issued by the President of the United States, I hereby assume command of the Army of the Potomac. Patriotism, and the exercise of my every energy in the direction of this army, aided by the full and hearty co-operation of its officers and men, will, I hope, under the blessing of God, insure its success. Having been a sharer of the privations, and a witness of the bravery of the old Army of the Potomac in the Maryland campaign, and fully identified with them in their feelings of respect and esteem for General McClellan, entertained through a long and most friendly association with him, I feel that it is not as a stranger I assume command... A. E. BURNSIDE, Major General Commanding." Our illustration represents the general issuing orders to his staff immediately after assuming command.

"The Forlorn Hope" — Volunteer Storming Party Crossing The Rappahannock In Advance Of The Grand Army, To Drive Off The Confederate Riflemen, Wednesday, December 10th, 1862.

We illustrate one of those numerous acts of daring which have raised the character of the Federal soldier to the highest position in the military world. General Burnside called for 100 volunteers to cross and dislodge, at the bayonet's point, concealed enemy sharpshooters. Thousands sprang forward, but only the number required was chosen. These consisted of men from the Seventh Michigan and Nineteenth Massachusetts Regiments. With the utmost alacrity this gallant "forlorn hope" sprang into the boats, and, on reaching the other side, drove the Confederates from their posts at the point of the bayonet, capturing 37 prisoners.

Passage Of The Rappahannock By The Grand Army Of The Potomac At Fredericksburg, Va.

The crossing over of the Federal army, on December 10th, 1862, was a most striking scene. Although a slight mist shrouded the lower part of the scene, floating a few feet above the river, the moonlight was resplendent. The shore was crowded with troops, while the glimmer of the bayonets and the camp fires made a picture never to be forgotten.

The Congressional Medal of Honor, the highest United States military decoration, was issued for the first time during the Civil War. More than 1,500 Medals of Honor were presented to soldiers and sailors during, and in the years after, the war.

Heroic Conduct Of Lieutenant Colonel Morrison, Seventy-ninth New York Highlanders, Leading
The Attack On The Parapet Of The Tower Battery, James Island, S. C.

THE UNION REFUSES
TO YIELD AFTER DEFEAT

Even the Fredericksburg disaster could not bring the
Federal government to its knees. In January 1863,
Burnside was replaced by General Hooker, nicknamed
"Fighting Joe." Hooker reshaped the Army of the
Potomac, as *Leslie's* wrote:

> The army was then reorganized, and many changes
> and dismissals of officers were made to secure obe-
> dience and competency.

The most important change was the consolidation of
Hooker's cavalry into a powerful force of twelve thousand
horsemen.

Other crucial campaigns and battles had taken
place elsewhere. In October 1862 Confederate general
Braxton Bragg, with sixty thousand men, was defeated
at Perryville, Kentucky, by General D.C. Buell's army of
sixty-five thousand. War continued along the Mississippi,
the Arkansas, and other strategic rivers, and Federal operations were continuing along the coast of the Carolinas,
where Confederate strongholds were being attacked and
captured one by one. ★

A Sutler's Store, Harpers Ferry, Va. — From A Sketch By Our Special Artist.

The sutler's store at Harpers Ferry represents one of those apparently inevitable evils which attend even the best-arranged armies. As a study of human life, a sutler's store is full of the most sorrowful reflections, and demands the most earnest care of the superior officers. A little pure stimulant, when administered with the rations, is capable of warding off many ills which flesh is heir to, more especially when under the prostration of fatigue or privation.

SOLDIERS' LETTERS

Northern troops could buy special stamps and envelopes to make sending letters home inexpensive. The Civil War was one of the most literary wars in history—profusely written about in its time, and the American conflict most written about by historians in the following century and a half. Because so many Americans were literate, thousands of articulate and revealing soldiers' letters and journals from North and South have become a rich resource of first-person descriptions of the Civil War.

Express Office At Fortress Monroe, Va. — Receiving Letters And Packages From Home In 1861.

Anyone who had relatives in camp knew the feverish anxiety of the troops to hear from those they had left at home. We need hardly describe a scene which so thoroughly explains itself. The name of the shipping company, Adams Express, was a household one, both to donor and receiver of good things that were sent to the soldiers.

The Hurricane Deck Of The United States Transport "North Star" — Soldiers Of The Forty-first Massachusetts Regiment Writing Home, Upon Arrival At Ship Island, Gulf Of Mexico.

We publish a sketch taken on the evening of the arrival of this Massachusetts regiment at Ship Island in 1862.

Thoughts of dear ones at home were uppermost on every soldier's mind, and in a very short time the hurricane deck

of the steamer North Star *was occupied by a regiment of letter-writers, all hard at work.*

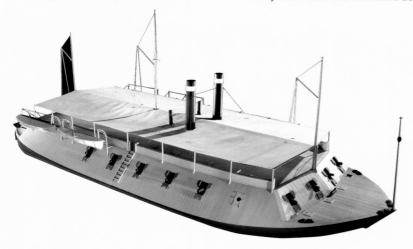

The USS *Carondelet* was typical of the ironclads used to penetrate rivers in support of Union land forces during the Civil War. Federal troops stationed along waterways—whether in the Gulf of Mexico or on the Virginia coast at Fortress Monroe and Norfolk—felt secure when these gunboats were on hand. Gunboats also carried mail to and from front-line troops. This scale model was built according to the original plans.

CHAPTER 5

WAR ON RIVER AND COAST

Surprise And Capture Of The Gunboat "Harriet Lane" By The Confederates, And Destruction Of The "Westfield."

About two o'clock in the morning of January 1st, 1863, Federal gunboats at Galveston were attacked by five Confederate steamers loaded with troops armed with rifles, muskets, etc. The Harriet Lane was captured by boarding after about all of her officers, including Captain Wainwright and Lieutenant Commander Lee, and a crew of 130, all told, had been killed by musketry from the Confederate steamers. The gunboats Clifton and Owasco escaped, and the squadron's flagship, Westfield, appeared about to fall into enemy hands when her captain blew her up. By some mismanagement or accident the explosion took place before he and some crew members got away, and they were blown up with the ship.

Combat Between The Confederate Ram "Arkansas" And The Federal Gunboat "Carondelet."

On July 15th, 1862, the gunboats Carondelet and Tyler encountered the enormous Confederate iron-plated ram Arkansas fifteen miles above Vicksburg. Captain Walke of the Carondelet ordered the Tyler to proceed at all speed to alarm the fleet while he engaged the Confederate monster. The Carondelet commenced with her bow guns, but without effect on the iron plating. Captain Walke ran the Carondelet alongside the Arkansas and the order "Boarders away!" was instantly passed. The crew of the Federal gunboat speedily mounted the deck of its adversary but found no foe to engage. The crew of the Arkansas had retired below, and the iron hatches were closed, so that it was utterly impossible to continue the action. The boarders returned to their vessel, and the Arkansas proceeded downriver toward the federal fleet.

IN 1862 ADMIRAL DAVID FARRAGUT planned the capture of Vicksburg, Mississippi, and Port Hudson, Louisiana, Confederate strongholds that prevented free navigation of the Mississippi River. Vicksburg, on high ground, was the more strongly fortified, and its guns dominated the river.

Late that spring, Federal forces captured Baton Rouge, Louisiana, and made it possible for Farragut to pass upriver to Vicksburg. His gunboats opened a bombardment of the Vicksburg batteries, but without effect. The capture of the city would require a regular siege by land forces. In the course of this campaign, the powerful Confederate ram *Arkansas* came from its base in the Yazoo River and daringly fought its way through the Union fleet to the shelter of Vicksburg's guns.

Early in August, a Confederate force attempted to regain possession of Baton Rouge, and the *Arkansas* went downriver in support. Before she reached Baton Rouge, however, her machinery broke down, and she became unmanageable and had to be run ashore. The commander set the *Arkansas* ablaze to prevent capture. The overland attack on Baton Rouge also failed.

Fighting continued in Arkansas and Missouri, where Confederate guerrilla forces roamed almost at will until General J. M. Schofield dispersed them and also defeated Confederate troops attempting to concentrate in Missouri. Union forces began to occupy eastern Texas, and the port city of Galveston fell in October. Late that month the Confederates were defeated at Labadieville, Louisiana. Much of this region, militarily designated the Department of the Gulf, was brought under Federal control, with General N. P. Banks taking command.

Toward the close of 1862 Union general W. S. Rosecrans and his Army of the Cumberland reached Stones River, near Murfreesboro, Tennessee. On the opposite side of the river, within cannon shot, lay Confederate general Braxton Bragg's army, reorganizing after defeat at Perryville. On December 31 the Battle of Stones River (also called Murfreesboro) began and continued for three days. Repeated Confederate assaults were met with Union determination, and after much bloodshed Bragg withdrew, marching his army southward. Of the Union's more than forty-one thousand men in action, almost twelve thousand were casualties; the thirty-five thousand Confederates engaged lost almost eleven thousand. ★

Banks's Expedition — Burning Baton Rouge,
La., During the Campaign of December 1862.

Battle Of Stones River, Tenn. — The Decisive Charge Of General Negley's Division Across The River — The Confederates Flying In Confusion From The Battlefield.

We question if a more spirited sketch was ever published than our engraving representing the final charge of General J. S. Negley's division, on the afternoon of Friday, January 2d, 1863, at the battle of Stones River. General Rosecrans, seeing that the critical moment had arrived, gave orders for General Negley to cross the river and drive the enemy from his position. Our artist reported: "The scene was grand in the extreme. Nothing could resist our gallant men; on they rushed; the Confederates met the shock, then wavered, and then were driven back at the bayonet's point, step by step, for some half-mile, when they broke and fled. Night fell on the scene, and the victors and vanquished rested from their strife."

GRANT ADVANCES ON VICKSBURG

At the end of 1862 Federal forces in the western theater prepared to take Vicksburg and Port Hudson. Grant would advance on Vicksburg by railroad with forty thousand men and unite with Sherman, whose thirty-two thousand men would pass downriver in transports guarded by Commodore Porter's gunboats.

A number of related actions opened the first phase of Grant's campaign for Vicksburg. Sherman was repulsed at Chickasaw Bayou on December 28 and retired to concentrate his force twelve miles above Vicksburg. Grant's force was harried by Confederate cavalry that destroyed supplies and tore up railroad track. In a separate expedition, Union general John A. McClernand attacked Fort Hindman on January 9, with support from Sherman. Porter's fleet of fifteen gunboats and fifty transports had carried McClernand's thirty thousand troops to Arkansas Post, fifty miles up the Arkansas River. They landed within three miles of the fort, and Porter's gunboats began a bombardment. The fort and almost five thousand defenders surrendered on January 12. McClernand then was put under Grant's command.

Grant was forced to conduct a prolonged siege of Vicksburg. Meanwhile, another Confederate force was assembling eastward to come to Vicksburg's relief. Grant decided to attack that force. In March,

Porter ran by the batteries at Vicksburg with nearly his whole fleet and a number of transports, which were protected from shot by bales of cotton and hay. These transports were manned by volunteers, which led Grant to say, in one of his reports: It is a striking feature of the volunteer army of the United States that there is nothing which men are called upon to do, mechanical or professional, that accomplished adepts cannot be found for the duty required, in almost every regiment.

The gunboats and transports then ferried Grant's troops—which had marched down the opposite shore, past Vicksburgh—back across to the east side of the river. Grant took Port Gibson on May 1 after a short battle and prepared to move on Jackson, Mississippi's capital. ★

Field glasses of General Ulysses S. Grant. Through these glasses were seen some of the most momentous events of the war.

The Investment Of Fort Hindman, Arkansas Post, Ark., And Its Bombardment By Rear Admiral D. D. Porter's Federal Gunboats, January 11th, 1863.

Fort Hindman was what is known in military parlance as a star fort, with four angles—two on the river and two extending nearly to the morass in the rear. In front of the southwestern angle was a cluster of small houses, into which the enemy had thrown their sharpshoot-ers, and from which a most galling fire was poured upon Federal troops, who stormed them and carried them by assault. For three long hours they fought ere the houses were carried. All that, while sharpshooters were picking the Federal troops off, and Parrott guns were sending their hissing messengers of death through the lines of the devoted attackers, crushing bones, spattering brains, and strewing the path with mangled corpses and dying men.

Towing Wounded Federal Soldiers On A Raft After Battle In Louisiana.

General Banks had arranged to stop the depredations which the Confederate steamer J. A. Cotton had been long committing along Louisiana's Bayou Teche. He had advanced from Labadieville on January 11th, 1863, with four gunboats, ten regiments of infantry and one of artillery. Their progress was stopped by earthworks, under whose guns lay the J. A. Cotton. Early on the 15th the gunboats opened fire, while the troops were advancing on shore to engage the Confederate vessels and batteries from the rear. The J. A. Cotton finally had to retire toward Butte La Rose, on the Atchafalaya. Early on the following morning the J. A. Cotton was seen floating down the bayou in a sheet of flame, having been set afire and abandoned by the Confederates. Meanwhile, the Federal wounded had been placed on a raft and towed down the river by a gunboat that brought them safely to a hospital.

Battle Of Baker's Creek, May 1863 — Defeat Of The Confederates By General Grant.

On May 16th General Grant met General J. C. Pemberton, with the whole garrison of Vicksburg, at Baker's Creek, and defeated him, driving him back toward Vicksburg, with a loss of 29 pieces of artillery and 4,000 men, and cutting him off from all hopes of relief. Pressing rapidly on, Grant, on the 17th, overtook Pemberton at Big Black River Bridge, and again defeated him, with a loss of 2,600 men and 17 guns. Pemberton then retired into the city.

GRANT TAKES VICKSBURG

Sherman joined Grant on May 8, and the combined force started for Jackson, Mississippi, about forty-five miles east of Vicksburg. There on May 14, Grant's troops engaged several thousand troops under Joseph Johnston, who had just arrived to take command of Confederate forces in the region. Grant's movements had cut Johnston off from Vicksburg.

After a short battle Johnston withdrew northward. Grant left Sherman to destroy captured war matériel and marched to Champion Hill, where General John C. Pemberton, Vicksburg's commander, had arrived with twenty-two thousand men. Grant was waiting for reinforcements, but on May 16 he sent his twenty-nine thousand troops on the attack. Pemberton was driven from the field, pursued and again defeated, and sent in retreat toward Vicksburg.

Siege Of Vicksburg — Life In The Trenches.

Our illustration shows the life led by the besieging Federal troops before the stronghold of Vicksburg. The deep ravine is studded with rude huts, or quarters, burrowed in the earth near the White house, which is well-riddled with Confederate shell. To the left of the house an opening in the bank shows the entrance to the "covered way" by which the Confederate works were approached.

Siege Of Vicksburg — The Fight In The Crater Of Fort Hill After The Explosion, June 27th, 1863.

The city of Vicksburg is in the distance. The entire crest, with the exception of this point, was held by the Confederates. Positioned here, Federal sharpshooters were protected by gabions *filled with earth, on top of which were placed heavy logs, with small portholes, through which they kept up a continuous fire. This fire decided the siege. The key of the Confederate works had been* *carried, and Pemberton, after a fruitless endeavor to obtain terms, surrendered to Grant's victorious army on the fourth of July, Independence Day, 1863.*

Grant swept on to Vicksburg's door and, believing Pemberton's troops must be demoralized, tried twice to take the city by storm. The second and largest assault was on May 22, when almost his whole army attacked simultaneously. Pemberton was ready.

The frowning fortifications became almost a mass of flame as they poured forth a deadly fire upon the uncovered troops below. Bravely the army struggled, with terrible loss of life, to gain a foothold where they could stop the murderous guns. . . . The broken army was at length compelled to fall back and abandon the struggle.

Day after day, Grant's batteries on land and water bombarded the city, driving defenders and inhabitants into caves dug in the earth. As weeks passed, famine and sickness plagued Vicksburg. While projectiles were dropping onto the city and its fortifications, Union engineers dug tunnels nearer and nearer that undermined Confederate defensive works. More than a ton of explosives was placed beneath one fort, which was blown up on June 25. A second mine was exploded a few days later.

On July 4, 1863, with all hope gone, Pemberton at last surrendered Vicksburg and thirty-seven thousand men. ★

Bombardment Of Port Hudson, La., By Admiral Farragut's Fleet.

Assault Of The Second Louisiana Colored Regiment On The Confederate Works
At Port Hudson, Louisiana, May 27th, 1863.

PORT HUDSON FALLS TO BANKS

Grant's campaign was one of the war's most brilliant military triumphs. It included victory in several battles in the field, the occupation of Jackson, Mississippi's capital, and the capture of Vicksburg, the strongest defensive position on the Mississippi River.

The Confederacy lost at least ten thousand killed and wounded (among the killed were three generals), and forty thousand prisoners, including fifteen generals. Grant's casualties were estimated at eighty-five hundred. The South lost arms and munitions for an army of sixty thousand and a large amount of other property, consisting of railroad locomotives and cars, steamboats, and tons of cotton. Further, much had been destroyed just to keep it from Grant.

In the meantime Banks had invested Port Hudson, which was under the command of General Frank Gardner. Late in May, with the assistance of Farragut's squadron and mortar boats, Banks began a siege. As did Grant at Vicksburg, Banks made two disastrous and bloody attempts to breach the defenses by frontal assault. Among the most valiant attacks were the charges of the Union's new black regiments raised in Louisiana. Known as Louisiana Native Guards, these were the first regiments of black soldiers to see major action in the war. They were admired and praised by the white troops who watched them in action or who fought alongside them.

These attacks all failed, and the siege continued until a shortage of ammunition and food and the fall of Vicksburg made it impossible to hold Port Hudson. On July 9 Gardner surrendered. The Federals lost three thousand men, the Confederates seventy-two hundred, including fifty-five hundred prisoners.

The capture of Vicksburg and Port Hudson sent a thrill of joy throughout the North, for in it the people of the loyal States could see signs of the early ending of the war. The loss of these important places would be a blow to the Confederacy from which it could never recover. Grant was hailed as a great general and took a high place in the regard of the people. ★

THE WOUNDED AND THEIR CARE

Mid-nineteenth-century battle wounds were often fatal because medicine was primitive and sanitation and sterilization were hardly known or practiced. Militaries and governments struggled to care for the wounded. There were a few poorly trained "surgeons" in each regiment, but the wounded were better cared for by their army's civilian "camp followers"—often members of their own families.

The newly established British Sanitary Commission's unprecedented success at saving soldiers' lives in the Crimean War (1853–56) inspired Americans to create their own Sanitary Commission during the Civil War. Private citizens on the Union side operated the Sanitary Commission, raising funds, building hospitals, and even tending soldiers near the battlefields.

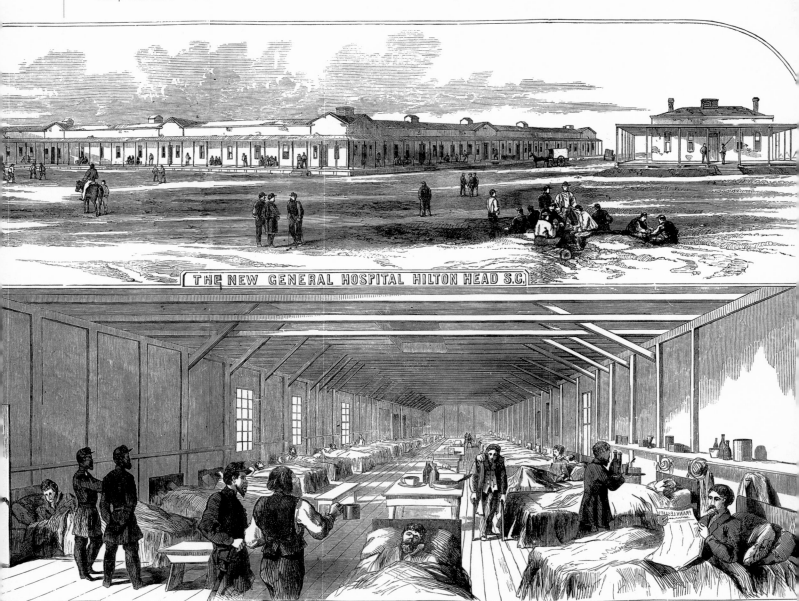

THE NEW GENERAL HOSPITAL HILTON HEAD S.C.

United States General Hospital, Hilton Head, S. C. — Exterior And Interior

The United States General Hospital at Hilton Head, S.C., was built very strongly of wood, and really had somewhat of an architectural appearance. It was about four hundred feet long, and had excellent accommodation for about five hundred patients. On the right hand of the hospital is the chief doctor's residence. We also publish a view of one of the wards, taken shortly after the battle of James Island, where so many Federals fell, either killed or wounded.

Naval Hospital And Battery At Portsmouth, Va.

The Confederate Batteries Shelling The Federal Position On The Night Of The Battle Of Cedar Mountain, August 9, 1862 — Wounded Men Lying On The Ground, As Other Troops Advance.

The scene at night was very striking. It was past ten o'clock, and there was a bright moonlight and a clear blue sky. The Federal troops were on a rising ground, while the enemy's batteries were shelling from the woods, Federal batteries replying, and one by one driving them further back. The hospital was near the Federal position, and wounded men were lying on the ground, waiting their turn to receive surgical attention. Near them were groups of stragglers, ambulances, and the army's supply and ammunition wagons, etc.

LESLIE'S GALLERY OF UNION OFFICERS

Leslie's artists made portraits of many leading Union officers to illustrate feature articles and to accompany descriptions of ongoing campaigns, but Confederate commanders seldom became their subjects. For years after the war, Northerners often considered Southern commanders to have been traitors rather than heroic soldiers. It was the victorious Union general officers who held the limelight in *Leslie's* pages. Following are abbreviated descriptions adapted from longer captions describing the careers of these commanders, many of them famous in the Northern states during their lifetimes. There were 1,978 Union general officers in the course of the war, with U. S. Grant as the only lieutenant general. The rest were major generals or brigadier generals. There were 80 full major generals and 197 full brigadier generals; more than 1,700 were temporary, or brevet, generals.

William T. Sherman
Born in Ohio in 1818, General Sherman graduated from West Point. After capturing Atlanta and making his famous march to the sea, he pushed northward, contributing to Lee's surrender.

Irvin McDowell
Major General McDowell was born in Ohio in 1818. An 1838 West Point graduate, he commanded the first Union army but was defeated at the Battle of Bull Run.

W.S. Rosecrans
Brigadier General Rosecrans was born in Ohio in 1819, and graduated West Point in 1842. His first important action was a victory at Rich Mountain in 1861.

Don Carlos Buell
Major General Buell, born in Ohio in 1818, graduated West Point in 1841. A career soldier, he helped Grant in gaining for the Federals the battle of Shiloh.

J.K.F. Mansfield
General Mansfield was born in 1803 in Connecticut. Graduating West Point in 1822, he became a professional soldier. A Union corps commander, he died from wounds after Antietam in 1862.

Nathaniel Lyon
General Lyon was born in 1819 in Connecticut and graduated West Point in 1841. He commanded the U.S. arsenal at St. Louis, and in 1861 died at Wilson's Creek.

Frémont's cavalry ford the Osage River at Warsaw, Mo., in October 1861.

Samuel D. Sturgis

General Sturgis, born in Pennsylvania in 1822, graduated West Point in 1846 and served in the Mexican War. He fought at South Mountain, Antietam, and Fredericksburg.

Darius N. Couch

Born in New York in 1822, General Couch graduated West Point in 1846 and served in the Mexican War. He fought at Fair Oaks, Williamsburg, Malvern Hill, Antietam, Fredericksburg, and Chancellorsville.

Philip H. Sheridan

General Philip H. Sheridan, born in New York in 1831, became a West Point graduate. In 1864 he took command of the Army of the Potomac's cavalry corps.

Daniel E. Sickles

Born in New York City in 1823, General Sickles gained distinction at Williamsburg, Fair Oaks, Malvern Hill, and Chancellorsville. At Gettysburg he lost a leg but continued in active service.

John M. Schofield

General Schofield, born in New York in 1831, graduated West Point in 1853. He fought in Missouri and in the battles of Resaca, Dallas, Kenesaw Mountain, Atlanta, and Franklin.

John F. Reynolds

General Reynolds was born in Pennsylvania in 1820, graduated West Point in 1843, and served in the Mexican War. A key Union general officer, he was killed at Gettysburg.

John Sedgwick

General Sedgwick, born in Connecticut in 1813, was an 1837 graduate of West Point and first served in the cavalry. He was killed by a sharpshooter at Spotsylvania Courthouse in 1864.

David D. Porter

Admiral Porter, born in Pennsylvania in 1813, entered the U. S. Navy as a midshipman in 1829. During the war, he served in key river and coastal campaigns and became a vice admiral.

Winfield Scott Hancock

General Hancock, born in Pennsylvania in 1824, graduated West Point in 1844 and became a career officer. He served in all the major eastern campaigns despite a severe wound at Gettysburg.

George G. Meade

Major General Meade, born in Spain in 1815, was an 1835 graduate of West Point and one of the first Union generals. He led the army to victory at Gettysburg.

John A. Logan

General Logan, born in Illinois in 1826, raised an infantry regiment in 1861 and rose from colonel to major general of volunteers in command of a division.

James B. McPherson

General McPherson, born in Ohio in 1828, died in action near Atlanta in 1864. An 1853 West Point graduate, he served with Grant and Sherman and won rapid promotion.

Military Buildings Erected On Hilton Head, S. C. — Commissary's Quarters And Regimental Camps.

George H. Thomas

General Thomas, born in Virginia in 1816, was an 1840 West Point graduate. He served with great distinction in the Department of the Cumberland to the close of the war.

Hugh J. Kilpatrick

General Kilpatrick, born in New Jersey in 1836, graduated West Point in 1861 and eventually became a cavalry commander. He was brevetted—promoted—for gallantry, and rose to major general.

George A. Custer

General Custer, born in Ohio in 1839, graduated West Point in 1861. A cavalryman, he became a brigadier general, noted for gallantry, from Bull Run to the end of the war.

Lewis Wallace

General Wallace, born in Indiana in 1827, fought as an infantry lieutenant in the Mexican War. He rose to major general of volunteers, serving in the eastern and western theaters.

George Crook

General Crook, an 1852 West Point graduate, was born in Ohio in 1828. He became a cavalry commander and took part in numerous Civil War actions in Tennessee and Virginia.

Benjamin F. Butler

General Butler was born in New Hampshire in 1818. A militia general, he led the Eighth Massachusetts Regiment to the first defense of Washington, D. C., in April 1861.

Alfred Pleasonton

General Pleasonton, born in Washington, D. C., in 1824, graduated West Point in 1844 and served in the Mexican War. He was an outstanding cavalry commander.

Rutherford B. Hayes

General Hayes, who became nineteenth President of the United States, was born in Ohio in 1822. He rose from major to general for his distinguished service in Virginia campaigns.

James A. Garfield

General Garfield, twentieth President of the United States, was born in Ohio in 1831. A general by 1863, he resigned to serve in Congress, having been elected fifteen months before.

Jesse L. Reno
General Reno, born in West Virginia in 1823, graduated West Point in 1846, and served in Mexico. A Union corps commander, he was killed in the 1862 Antietam campaign.

Fitzjohn Porter
General Porter was born in New Hampshire in 1822 and graduated West Point in 1846. In 1863, he was unjustly cashiered for disobeying orders, but years later was exonerated and reinstated.

Robert H. Milroy
General Milroy, born in Indiana in 1816, served in the Mexican War as a captain. An attorney, he enlisted in 1861 and rose to major general in command of a division.

Chester A. Arthur
General Arthur, twenty-first President of the United States, was born in Vermont in 1830. A New York militia officer in 1861, he served as inspector general and quartermaster general.

John Buford
General Buford was born in Kentucky in 1825. Graduating West Point in 1848, he served as a dragoon until the war. He commanded the Army of the Potomac's cavalry.

Joseph Hooker
General Hooker, born in Massachusetts in 1814, graduated West Point in 1837. A key Union general, he commanded the Army of the Potomac at Chancellorsville in 1863, losing to Lee.

George Stoneman
General Stoneman was born in New York in 1822, graduated West Point in 1846, and joined the dragoons. He commanded Union cavalry in numerous campaigns until captured in 1864.

David G. Farragut
Admiral Farragut, born in Tennessee in 1801, was a midshipman by 1810 and served in the navy more than fifty years. His Gulf Squadron captured New Orleans in 1862.

Oliver O. Howard
General Howard, born in Maine in 1830, graduated West Point in 1854. He resigned for a field command, fought in many campaigns, and was twice wounded.

Steam-powered Federal Vessels Lie Quietly At Anchor Off The Norfolk, Va., Naval Base.

John Pope

Born in Kentucky in 1822, General Pope graduated West Point in 1842, serving in Florida and Mexico. As a Union field army commander he lost Second Bull Run in 1862.

Edwin V. Sumner

General Sumner, born in Massachusetts in 1797, entered the army in 1819. A corps commander who fought from the Peninsula to Fredericksburg, he died of wounds and illness in 1863.

Benjamin H. Grierson

General Grierson was born in Pennsylvania in 1826 and raised in Ohio. He led volunteer cavalry in the western theater, from Tennessee to Baton Rouge, including in the Vicksburg siege.

Benjamin Harrison

Born in Ohio in 1833, General Benjamin Harrison became twenty-third President of the United States. An attorney in 1861, he was commissioned colonel of volunteers, and rose to brigadier general.

John E. Wool

General Wool, born in New York in 1789, was a distinguished veteran of the War of 1812 and the Mexican War. A staff officer, he was the fourth-ranking general in the army.

Samuel F. du Pont

Born in New Jersey, Admiral du Pont was a midshipman by 1815. He commanded naval operations until declining health compelled him to serve on boards and commissions. He died in 1865.

CHAPTER 6
THE NORTHERN TIDE RISES

Conrad's Ferry, Md., Above Harrison's Island, On The Potomac River.

Conrad's Ferry, on the Maryland side of the upper Potomac, about five miles above Edward's Ferry, is shown in the *possession of Federal troops. It is immediately opposite to Leesburg Heights, about five miles from the Ferry, on the* *south side of the Potomac. This river often flowed between the opposing armies of North and South.*

The Crew Of The United States Gunboat "Mahaska," Captain Foxhall A. Parker, Destroying The Water Battery Built By The Confederates At West Point, Va., On The York River.

A Bridge "On The March" — Federal Wagons Laden With Pontoons To Build Floating Bridges Make Their Way From Acquia Creek To The Rappahannock In Northern Virginia.

FOR NEARLY THREE MONTHS after the battle of Fredericksburg in December 1862, the one hundred thirty-four thousand men of the Army of the Potomac remained inactive on the northern side of the Rappahannock River, near Fredericksburg. Lee's army, fortified on the south side of the river, numbered just sixty thousand, because a large detachment under General Longstreet had been detailed to forage for food in the countryside to supply the hungry Confederate army.

During these months Federal gunboats were active in support of operations against Confederate positions along the Virginia rivers and Chesapeake Bay. Other than this, only cavalry movements produced any actions of note. Early in February 1863 the Federals at Gloucester, Virginia, were raided by cavalry under General Fitzhugh Lee, and in March the Union garrison at Fairfax Courthouse was surprised in the middle of the night by mounted rangers led by Colonel John S. Mosby.

The first real cavalry contest of the war occurred on March 17, an engagement between twenty-one hundred men from the Union's Second Cavalry Division led by General William W. Averell and eight hundred cavalry under General Fitzhugh Lee. They met at Kelley's Ford, on the Rappahannock, and after a daylong battle the result was a stalemate. Averell withdrew, concerned that Confederate infantry reinforcements were on the way. This clash would be the first of increasingly larger cavalry battles.

In April, Hooker put his army in motion to force Lee out of his Fredericksburg positions. He sent General George Stoneman's ten thousand cavalry to destroy railroads and bridges on Lee's supply lines. Hooker planned to compel Lee to withdraw from Fredericksburg while cutting him off from supplies and transportation. Next, while General John Sedgwick prepared to engage Lee in front, Hooker took sixty thousand troops across the Rappahannock several miles above Fredericksburg.

At Chancellorsville, a hamlet in the densely forested region known as the Wilderness, Hooker began to entrench his army, expecting Lee to attack. He placed O. O. Howard's corps on his extreme right, with D. E. Sickles next to him, H. W. Slocum in the center, and G. G. Meade and D. N. Couch on the left. Now Lee took the initiative to attack and surprise Hooker. Leaving General J. A. Early with ten thousand men to face Sedgwick, Lee moved with forty-three thousand troops toward Hooker. On May 1 "Stonewall" Jackson took a force of twenty-six thousand to outflank Hooker's right wing. ★

Federal Cavalry Leaders — Generals Pleasonton, Bayard, And Colonel Percy Wyndham Making A Reconnaissance Near Fredericksburg, Va., In Preparation For A Campaign.

CHANCELLORSVILLE: ANOTHER UNION DEFEAT

Throughout the day on May 2, Jackson followed a local guide on a sixteen-mile march through the Wilderness, concealed from the Federals by the forest. At 6 P.M. his command prepared to attack the position of General Howard, an able commander who had lost an arm in the Peninsular campaign. Howard heard reports of a Confederate movement but did not believe it was a major threat.

Reaching Howard's position, [Jackson's force] suddenly burst from the woods upon him. Fierce and terrible was the onslaught, crushing the Federal column like an eggshell, and driving its broken pieces back upon the remainder of the line. In vain did the gallant Howard gallop furiously among his panic-stricken men and wave his empty sleeve as a banner to them. His column was wrecked, and he could not save it. Back it fell, and Jackson was about to gain the army's rear. But Hooker, taking in his peril at a glance, sent his old division, then [H. G.] Berry's, to the rescue. Presenting a solid front to the enemy, it enabled Sickles and Howard to rally their troops behind it, and Jackson's victorious course was checked. But, regardless of the terrific loads of canister that poured into their ranks from thirty pieces of artillery massed in front of Berry's position, the Confederates continued their attack until late in the evening.

As evening came on, Hooker attempted to form stronger defensive positions, and Jackson rode with his staff over the ground in front of his skirmishers, planning a night attack to cut off Hooker's retreat. As Jackson was returning to the lines in the darkness, his own men mistook him and his staff for Federal cavalry and opened fire. Jackson was gravely wounded, and Lee lost one of his most successful lieutenants that night, with the Battle of Chancellorsville still to be won. ★

Kelley's Ford, On The Rappahannock, The Scene Of The Battle Of The 17th Of March, 1863, And Of General Stoneman's Reconnaissance Of The 21st Of April.

A Scene From The Battle Of Chancellorsville, Va., Friday, May 1st, 1863.

We give a fine sketch of the point where the memorable battle of Chancellorsville began. It was at the junction of the Gordonsville Plank Road, the Old Turnpike, and the road from Ely's. The first fighting took place here on Friday, May 1st, and on Saturday the Eleventh Corps was routed, and the enemy repulsed by the most resolute bravery of the Federal troops. Here, too, on Sunday the enemy made an attack with such overwhelming numbers as to force the Federal army back to the second line. Few spots possess greater interest than this scene of fearful battle.

LEE'S MASTERPIECE

General J.E.B. Stuart took over the dying Jackson's troops, and at dawn the next morning, May 3, the battle was renewed with an attack on Sickles. During this battle, the concussion of a shell that exploded near Hooker put him temporarily out of action.

The Confederates were bravely met by the divisions of [D. B.] Birney and Berry, supported by forty pieces of artillery. For a time these made a stand . . . but the Confederates, undaunted by the heavy cannonading they received, dashed up at a furious pace and drove Sickles's corps gradually back, and after six hours' hard fighting they were pushed from the field to a strong position on the roads back of Chancellorsville.

While this struggle raged, Sedgwick crossed the Rappahannock and, after four repulses, captured the Fredericksburg heights that in December had seen the slaughter of so many Federals. Leaving a part of his force to hold these works, Sedgwick took his main army to join Hooker twelve miles away at Chancellorsville. Now Lee left Stuart with twenty-five thousand men to contain Hooker's seventy-five thousand and marched with twenty thousand to reinforce Early against Sedgwick, who was driven back across the river. Hooker soon retreated with the rest of his defeated army. The victory at Chancellorsville, called "Lee's masterpiece," cost the Federals more than seventeen thousand men, the Confederates almost thirteen thousand. ★

Battle Of Chancellorsville, Va. — Attack On General Sedgwick's Corps, May 4th, 1863, At 5 P. M., As Seen From Falmouth Heights.

After General Sedgwick had carried the fortifications on Sunday, May 3d, he pushed along the Gordonsville Plank in pursuit till night stopped his advance. Before morning the enemy threw a heavy force in his rear, cutting him off from his small force at Fredericksburg, and began to mass troops on his front and left flank. About half-past five o'clock in the afternoon they began the attack, and columns poured from behind the breastworks and marched down the hill to the plain above the town and opposite Falmouth, receiving, as they came in range, a brisk fire from the Federal artillery beyond the river. Unchecked by this, however, they rushed on Sedgwick's line, which repeatedly repulsed them, then fell back gradually to Banks's Ford and crossed in the morning on pontoons. In the sketch the breastworks captured on Sunday are seen, with the Confederates passing between them and the river in columns to attack Sedgwick's troops, which are the continuous line in the distance.

HOOKER'S HEAD QUARTERS CHANCELLORVILLE MAY 1ST

Battle Of Chancellorsville, May 3d, 1863 — General Hooker Repulsing The Attack Of The Enemy.

Early on May 3d Stuart renewed the attack upon Hooker's force, with the battle cry, "Charge, and remember Jackson!" and the advance was made with such impetuosity that in a short time he was in possession of the crest from which the Eleventh Corps had been driven the preceding day. No time was lost in crowning that eminence with all the heavy artillery obtainable, and as soon as this could be made to play upon the Federal lines a charge was successively ordered upon the position held by Generals Berry and French, both of whom were supported by the divisions of Williams and Whipple. After a severe struggle the Confederates succeeded in capturing the high ground where the Federals had posted some more heavy artillery. The enemy turned these guns upon the Federals, who soon had to fall back to their second and third lines of entrenchments. The Confederates followed close upon them, and made charge after charge in order to capture the new positions, but unavailingly, and when reinforcements arrived from Meade's corps they were forced to abandon the attack. Lee next turned against Sedgwick, who had captured Fredericksburg.

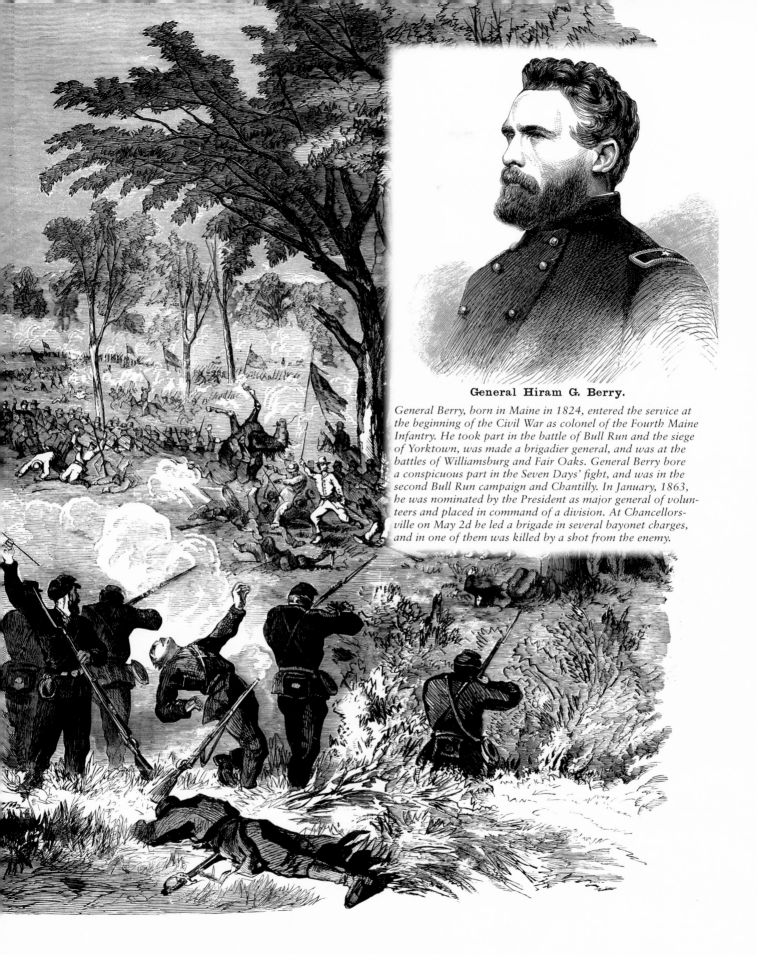

General Hiram G. Berry.

General Berry, born in Maine in 1824, entered the service at the beginning of the Civil War as colonel of the Fourth Maine Infantry. He took part in the battle of Bull Run and the siege of Yorktown, was made a brigadier general, and was at the battles of Williamsburg and Fair Oaks. General Berry bore a conspicuous part in the Seven Days' fight, and was in the second Bull Run campaign and Chantilly. In January, 1863, he was nominated by the President as major general of volunteers and placed in command of a division. At Chancellorsville on May 2d he led a brigade in several bayonet charges, and in one of them was killed by a shot from the enemy.

LEE STRIKES NORTH

Soon after the battle of Chancellorsville, Longstreet rejoined Lee after unsuccessfully operating against Federal positions in eastern Virginia in the hope of eventually seizing Norfolk and attacking Fortress Monroe. Longstreet's troops brought the Army of Northern Virginia's strength to eighty-nine thousand. Hooker had one hundred and twenty-two thousand troops positioned between Lee and Washington.

Lee now resolved to invade Maryland and carry the war into the North. His army was reorganized into three corps commanded by Longstreet, A.P. Hill, and Richard Ewell. On June 3, Lee sent his left wing, under Ewell, through the Shenandoah Valley, while Longstreet moved along the eastern base of the Blue Ridge Mountains. By June 25, Hill had followed, and the whole of Lee's army was in Maryland and Pennsylvania.

On June 27 General-in-Chief Halleck had a crucial disagreement with Hooker over the Army of the Potomac's next movements. As a result, Hooker resigned his command and was succeeded by George Meade, who moved against Lee.

Lee now determined to move upon Harrisburg and then push on to Philadelphia, but learning that Meade was well across the Potomac and was threatening his flank and rear, he decided to first concentrate his army at Gettysburg, and then deal such a demoralizing blow upon Meade that he could march on to Baltimore and Washington without trouble.

A.P. Hill's advance troops approached Gettysburg on July 1 and ran into General John Buford's cavalry. A sharp skirmish took place, and as the dismounted troopers fought against overwhelming numbers, Generals J. F. Reynolds and O. O. Howard hurried to their support. Reynolds was killed soon after reaching the field and was replaced by General Abner Doubleday.

When Ewell's corps appeared they outflanked the Federals, who retreated to strong positions on the nearby hills. General W.S. Hancock organized the Federal positions for the impending clash of the main armies.

[Meade] immediately dispatched orders to the different corps to march with utmost speed to Gettysburg, and then started off himself, reaching the place a little after midnight. Lee also concentrated his forces that night and prepared for the great battle of the morning. ★

Federal Troops Marching Back Into Falmouth, Va., After The Battle Of Chancellorsville.

Confederate Prisoners Brought In After The Battle Of Chancellorsville.

How The Daughters Of Maryland Received The Sons Of The North As They Marched Against
The Confederate Invaders — A Scene On The March.

MEADE STANDS FAST

Preparations for a major battle were being made as the morning of July 2, 1863, opened at Gettysburg, with troops arriving from every direction to reinforce the armies. Lee had seventy-five thousand to Meade's eighty-eight thousand.

Confederate attacks began in the late afternoon.

Longstreet made a fierce charge upon Meade's left, commanded by General Sickles. Amid the crash and thunder of artillery the Confederates dashed up savagely, but in splendid order, and dealt blow after blow, until the whole left wing of the Federals was shaken and gradually fell back. Just then the Fifth Corps, under [George] Sykes, came up and re-enforced Sickles. But this did not arrest the onslaught of the enemy; instead, the terrible fire of

the artillery that swept their ranks seemed to make them bolder and fiercer than ever.

The fight continued until ten o'clock in the evening, when the armies rested for the night. At four o'clock the next morning the battle was renewed on the Union right, with attacks and counterattacks. Lee's critical battle plan was to break through the Federal center. His massed artillery opened fire on the Union line, and fifteen thousand troops prepared to charge.

For two hours the country around shook with the reverberations. Then, at four o'clock, Lee ordered a grand charge. Gallantly his men obeyed the command. In splendid order they advanced rapidly in heavy columns. The steady hail of shot and shell

had no terrors for them; on they hurried, and even when the Federals, reserving their fire, poured a volley into their ranks that annihilated their first line, they still kept on, and dashing over the rifle pits and up to the guns, bayoneted or drove the gunners away. But . . . their triumphant charge was checked. The guns on the western slope of Cemetery Hill opened upon them with grape and canister with such awful effect [that] the Confederates [were] repulsed at every point. That night the field presented an awful sight, being covered with the dead bodies of men and horses.

The next day, July 4, Lee withdrew. He had suffered twenty-eight thousand casualties to the Federal loss of twenty-three thousand. ★

Battle Of Gettysburg — Cemetery Hill During The Attack Of The Confederates, Thursday Evening, July 2d, 1863.

No attack was made until about half-past three o'clock, when Lee ordered a simultaneous advance against each flank of the Federal army while demonstrations were being kept up against the centre. The attacks were not, however, made simultaneously, as Lee had intended. Longstreet began by sending Hood's force against Sickles's extreme left, then held by General Ward, whose three brigades extended their line from the Round Top across the Devil's Den, to and beyond the Peach Orchard, along the Emmittsburg Road. Ward's force was driven back after a bitter contest. Upon turning Ward's left Hood fell upon the flank and rear of Federal defenders, leading part of his force between that portion of the field and the Round Top, while other Confederates were also attacking nearby. The attack was made with such vigor that Sickles called for reinforcements, and three brigades were sent to him. A terrible struggle followed, and the ground was contested bitterly at all points.

Battle Of Gettysburg — Charge Of The Confederates On Cemetery Hill, Thursday, July 2d, 1863.

Confederate general Jubal Early makes an attempt to carry Cemetery Hill, after opening upon it with his massed artillery. He was beaten back and compelled to return to his original position before darkness had fairly set in.

Capture of Confederate Guns Near Culpeper By General Custer's Cavalry Brigade.

Federal cavalry went on the offense in the fall of 1863. General Alfred Pleasonton, on September 14th, 1863, drove the Confederates back on Culpeper, and General G. A. Custer with his brigade came up with enemy horse artillery, which he charged twice, himself at the head, and the second time took guns, limbers, horses and men. His horse was killed by a round shot, which wounded the general in the leg and killed a bugler behind him.

General Alexander S. Webb.

General Webb, born in New York City in 1835, graduated from West Point in 1855, and was assigned to the artillery. He served in Florida and Minnesota, and for three years as assistant professor at West Point. He was present at Bull Run and participated in the battles of the Pennsylvania campaign of the Army of the Potomac, and as chief of staff of the Fifth Corps during the Maryland and Rappahannock campaign. He was commissioned brigadier general of volunteers, serving with great credit at the Battle of Gettysburg. He eventually was made major general, United States Army, for gallant and meritorious services during the war.

STALEMATE IN VIRGINIA

The defeated Lee held Federal pursuit at bay and again took up a defensive position beyond the Rapidan River. Coupled with the fall of Vicksburg to Grant, Meade's victory at Gettysburg brought an outpouring of joy in the North. According to *Leslie's*:

> So great was the importance of the battle of Gettysburg that the triumph of the Federal army moved the President of the United States to recommend the observance of August 15th as a day of thanksgiving.

Lee detached Longstreet's corps, which went to reinforce Bragg at Chickamauga, Georgia, and two Union corps were sent westward under Hooker. As Meade and Lee maneuvered to gain advantage, there were infantry skirmishes and cavalry clashes but few battles of any consequence. The armies in northern Virginia went into winter quarters. ★

Edward's Ferry, Md., Below Harrison's Island, On The Potomac River.

Winter Quarters On The Rappahannock — Army Huts Of The One Hundred And Nineteenth
Regiment, Pennsylvania Volunteers, Near Falmouth, Va.

Going Into Camp At Stafford's Store, Va. — Third Brigade, Third Division, Sixth Corps, Carrying
Off Fence Rails From Farm Fields And Homes, And Gathering Persimmons.

Stafford's store is on the road from New
Baltimore to Falmouth, and had attached to it a meadow of about an acre,
entirely surrounded with a rail fence,
which was somewhat unusual in Virginia. Federal troops found it to be a place
where the supplies were more abundant
than in other districts; there were heard
the cackling of hens, the crowing of
roosters, the bleating of sheep, and all
those pleasant sounds so suggestive of
a good larder. Our artist significantly
added that those sounds would be heard
no more, plainly intimating that our
hungry soldiers made their originators
go the way of all flesh. It was a curious
sight to see the Federal soldiers each pull
up a rail and shoulder it. Before long,
therefore, the fence had disappeared,
leaving the field without the palisades.

IRON PANS AND HARDTACK

A soldier's winter shelter was not complete without his mess gear, which included a frying pan and cup, a lantern, and a small metal box to protect precious matches. Food was usually better in quarters than in the field, but there was always hardtack, the thick cracker that had to be soaked and softened before it could be eaten or mixed into stews or soups.

Civil War Soldier's Mess

Bivouac Of The Field And Staff Officers Of The Twelfth Massachusetts Regiment During A Stormy Night, On Their March From Hyattsville, Md.

CHAPTER 7

INSURRECTION, SIEGE, AND UNION ADVANCE

Siege Of Vicksburg — General Sherman's Fight With Hand Grenades, June 13th, 1863.

During the siege of Vicksburg there occurred a scene hitherto unparalleled in the Civil War. By two o'clock in the morning General Sherman's corps had pushed up to within twenty yards of a Confederate bastion. Cannon had now become useless to either party, and as musketry was of no avail, they had to resort to the hand grenade. The enemy threw lighted shells over the parapet onto the Federals, and received in return twenty-three hand grenades, which drove them out.

THE FALL OF VICKSBURG and victory at Gettysburg decisively turned the conflict in favor of the North in 1863, but the horrors of war had severely reduced the number of willing new volunteers. While many veteran soldiers reenlisted—being paid a bounty to do so—thousands more were desperately needed to carry the fight into the South. Now Congress authorized a draft wherever local enlistment boards did not meet their government-established quotas.

Compulsory conscription met with broad opposition, however, especially since wealthy men could pay for substitutes to take their places. The burden fell unfairly on those who could not afford to buy their way out of the draft. The white working classes of New York City were so inflamed that on July 13 they began to riot. For three days they wreaked havoc, attacking blacks, fighting police, and threatening to capture an arsenal full of firearms. Police aided by armed citizens held off the mob until the arrival of soldiers suppressed the insurrection. More than two hundred persons were killed, and property amounting to at least $2 million was destroyed.

At this time Confederate guerrilla John Morgan led a raid through Kentucky, southern Indiana, and Ohio, riding from village to village, plundering, destroying, and levying contributions. Morgan aimed to start an uprising of secessionists, but he was unsuccessful and soon was captured.

In Tennessee, the opposing armies of Rosecrans and Bragg prepared for battle, and cavalry forces on both sides were busy on scouts and raids. By June, Rosecrans had maneuvered toward Bragg, who occupied Chattanooga. When Bragg realized his supply lines were threatened, he withdrew from the city. In August, the advance elements of Rosecrans's Army of the Cumberland moved into Chattanooga and occupied the nearby heights, including Lookout Mountain.

Believing that Bragg was rapidly retreating, Rosecrans continued to advance. The Confederates turned, however, and readied an all-out attack on the unprepared Army of the Cumberland. By mid-September, the two armies were arrayed on opposite sides of Chickamauga Creek in northern Georgia, with Bragg about to take the offensive. ★

Cutting The Levees Near The State Line Of Louisiana And Arkansas, Twenty Miles Above Lake Providence, By Order Of General Grant During His 1863 Mississippi River Campaign.

Night Burial Of Colonel Garesche, Chief Of Staff To Major General Rosecrans, As Battle Rages.

We publish a most striking sketch, the temporary burying of one of the fallen Federal heroes, chief of staff to General Rosecrans, killed while serving at his side. Our artist thus describes this most emphatic scene: "No procession of plumed officers, no rolling of muffled drums, no parting volley of rattling musketry, none of the rites and ceremonies of religion. Alas! The living comrades of the dead hero cannot even turn aside to give a farewell glance at their departed friend. General Rosecrans and the friends of Garesche have their eyes strained upon the fight and dare not look back on the solemn group behind them. There stand some orderlies around the body of the fallen colonel. See how tenderly these rough and battle-scarred veterans perform their labor of love and sorrow. Their eyes are filled with tears, and not a word is spoken. There is no coffin, no shroud, no pall —it will be truly ashes and dust to dust. From the trees around they gather green cedar branches; over the poor clay they carefully lay these protecting boughs; and then, beneath the light of our flaming torch and a dim lantern, the earth is gently laid over the gallant Garesche."

The War In Virginia — Caissons And Horses After Action At Bristoe Station.

Flag Of Truce From The Confederates, To Bury Their Dead, At Port Royal, S. C.

BRAGG DEFEATS ROSECRANS AT CHICKAMAUGA CREEK

The Battle of Chickamauga opened on the morning of September 19, 1863, when the Confederates attacked the Federal left and drove it back. General George Thomas then led this wing in a counterattack that forced the Confederates back. Next the Federal center began giving way, but Thomas came up and rallied the troops.

The battle surged back and forth, and Bragg was foiled in every attempt to penetrate Rosecrans's line. After the armies broke off for the night, exhausted, Bragg was reinforced by troops of Longstreet's corps from northern Virginia. Longstreet himself also arrived that night, increasing Bragg's army to more than sixty-six thousand men, while Rosecrans had fifty-eight thousand.

The next morning, the battle was renewed with repeated Confederate charges probing for a weak spot in the Federal line. Then, by chance, Longstreet attacked at a point where a gap had appeared as Federal units were being shifted. Longstreet broke through and swept everything before him. Rosecrans himself was borne backward and fled to the safety of Chattanooga.

Thomas, however, held his ground as the Confederates rallied for a decisive blow. Thomas's ammunition was exhausted, and he had nothing to stop this last assault except the bayonet. So when the foe came on and reached striking distance he shouted "Give them the cold steel!" Forgetting their weariness, his men sprang forward and charged so quickly and steadily that the Confederates turned and fled, and the left wing of Rosecrans's army was saved.

The entire Federal army then fell back to Chattanooga, defeated, but Chickamauga cost the Confederates more than eighteen thousand casualties. Rosecrans, who lost more than sixteen thousand, was ordered to St. Louis and replaced by Grant. ★

The Raid In Kentucky — The Confederate Morgan.

General John H. Morgan.

General Morgan, born in Huntsville, Alabama, in 1826, served in the War with Mexico as a cavalry officer. He entered the Confederate Army and rose to be a general. During the winter of 1862–63 he commanded a cavalry force that greatly annoyed General Rosecrans's outposts and communications. In mid-1863, he raided into Kentucky, Ohio, and Indiana, but was captured and imprisoned in the Ohio Penitentiary. He soon escaped by digging his way out, and the following year raided into Tennessee. He was surrounded by Federal troops and killed trying to escape.

The Army Of The Cumberland — Wilder's Mounted Infantry Passing A Blockhouse On The Nashville And Chattanooga Railroad During The 1863 Tennessee Campaign.

Mounted infantry commanded by Colonel John T. Wilder appear in our engraving passing a blockhouse on the Nashville and Chattanooga Railroad. The mounted infantry brigade consisted of Colonel Wilder's regiment, the Seventeenth Indiana, the Seventy-second and Seventy-fifth Indiana, and Ninety-eighth Illinois. They were mounted by Colonel Wilder in order to enable him to cope with Morgan and other Confederate guerrillas. This step cost the government nothing, Colonel Wilder's horses and accoutrements being all captured from the enemy.

Battle Of Chickamauga, Ga., September 19th-20th, 1863, Between Generals Rosecrans And Bragg.

Our sketch of this most important battle shows General Thomas and his staff anxiously looking for reinforcements as his troops, from their temporary breastwork of logs and knapsacks, are *repulsing repeated Confederate assaults and saving the Army of the Cumberland from destruction. Although Thomas held his men together, the Confederates routed Rosecrans's main body. Thomas* *was reinforced and repulsed the enemy before falling back the next night, un-molested, toward Chattanooga. He won the nickname "Rock of Chickamauga."*

Battle Of Chickamauga — Repulse Of The Confederates At Crawfish Creek.

This sketch from the battle of Chickamauga illustrates the repulse of the
Confederate cavalry by the Twenty-
fourth Illinois and Company K of the
Nineteenth Illinois. They were separated
from the Confederates by a stone fence

and a small creek. Their daring and
heroic resistance was never surpassed,
some of them climbing the stone fence
to meet the Confederates rushing madly
down upon the little band. Notwithstanding vast odds, they held their

position until reinforcements reached
them. The Twenty-fourth Illinois went
into the battle with three hundred and
thirty men, and came out with fewer
than half that number.

General John B. Hood.

A graduate of West Point, Hood served on the frontier before resigning to join the Confederacy. A veteran commander in all the major eastern campaigns and wounded several times, Hood went with Longstreet to support Bragg. He lost a leg at Chickamauga, yet returned to command for the rest of the war.

IDENTIFICATION MEDALLION

These one-inch diameter lead or brass discs, with eagle and shield on one side, were suspended on a string or chain around the necks of Union soldiers. They would be inscribed with identifying information in case the wearer fell in battle.

U.S. GRANT ARRIVES TO SAVE CHATTANOOGA

After Chickamauga, the Army of the Cumberland at Chattanooga was besieged by Bragg, who occupied Missionary Ridge and Lookout Mountain, controlling the Tennessee River and cutting off supply from the northwest. Bragg's cavalry raids destroyed wagonloads of supplies from other directions and damaged the railroad lines.

Now the armies of the Cumberland and the Tennessee were consolidated under Grant, who hurried to Chattanooga. He put Thomas in charge of the Army of the Cumberland, and Sherman took over the Army of the Tennessee.

Grant wanted to reopen a supply route by taking full possession of Brown's Ferry on the Tennessee River three miles below Lookout Mountain. On the night of October 27, an expedition set out to seize the ferry landing held by Confederates on the other side of the river from Union forces. About fifteen hundred men loaded into pontoons and flatboats and pushed out into the stream. They drifted downriver in silence, without using oars, and passed unnoticed in front of Confederate sentinels on Lookout Mountain.

They soon made a landing, and while the boats were rowed across the river to a point where stood the balance of the 4,000 troops, who had secretly marched thither by land, a strong position to resist the now alarmed enemy was secured. When the whole force had disembarked the Confederates retreated up the valley, and the Federals took the opportunity of building a pontoon bridge that soon spanned the river and opened a way for re-enforcement and supplies.

Locomotives Built At Vicksburg, Miss., By Federal Soldiers, Under The Superintendence Of General McPherson's Staff.

Our special artist transmitting this sketch wrote: "I herein inclose a sketch of five locomotives just completed here, being the result of the mechanical ingenuity displayed by the men in this department. General Grant…[once] remarked that there was no department of mechanical labor required to be performed but that men were always on hand well skilled in the business. The completion of these fine specimens of workmanship affords ample proof of the truth of his remark. On entering the city, last July, we found the debris of a machine shop and some scattered fragments of locomotives. Out of these our men have created a good workshop, with all the necessary machinery for casting car wheels, etc., and the result stands forth in these engines…"

Lookout Mountain And Its Vicinity, From The Position Of The Eleventh Army Corps.

WAR IN TENNESSEE: LOOKOUT MOUNTAIN

Joining Grant at Chattanooga were experienced commanders from the Army of the Potomac, including Generals Hooker, Burnside, and Howard, who with their troops had come out swiftly by train. Hooker was ordered to menace Bragg's left flank and protect the passage of supplies up the Tennessee to the army at Chattanooga.

The Confederates attacked Hooker on October 29, and the Federals

had a severe struggle against overwhelming numbers, but being re-enforced, and the men being cheered by the presence of Hooker in the most critical places, the Confederates were at length driven away to the shelter of Lookout Mountain, after a three hours' battle in the darkness. During the contest about 200 mules, panic-stricken by the noise of the guns, dashed into the Confederate ranks, and the men, supposing it to be a charge of Hooker's cavalry, fell back in confusion for a moment.

U.S. GRANT'S COMMISSION
President Abraham Lincoln signed this document, which commissioned Ulysses S. Grant as a major general. It is officially dated July 4, 1863, the day Grant captured the key Confederate city of Vicksburg after a lengthy siege.

Federal Pickets Near Chattanooga Are Approached By Confederates Camouflaged In Cedar Bushes.

Our sketch shows the Confederate device for shooting down the Federal pickets. We have here single trees moving in the dusky twilight, continuously and stealthily, so that their onward movement may be taken for the mere swaying of the trees in the wind. But Federal pickets in the third year of the war were keen of eye and ear, and the hand on the trigger tells that some will fall in their cedar coffins to lie amid the crags and woods of that wild country.

Grant next sent Hooker to attack Lookout Mountain, and Sherman was directed to cross the Tennessee and strike Bragg's right at Missionary Ridge. On November 24 Hooker's men fought their way up the steep, rugged sides of the mountain, their subsequent victory concealed from onlookers in the valley below by a thick mist. The next day Sherman's force launched its attack, led by Thomas. Defying heavy artillery and rifle fire, the Union soldiers climbed up Missionary Ridge as rocks and boulders, and explosive shells with lighted fuses, rolled down at them. Grant himself looked on as his soldiers struggled to reach the summit, and they cheered in triumph as they drove Bragg's army away.

Even the stoic General Thomas was moved to see this victory, saying, "I did not think it possible for men to accomplish so much!"

The Federal loss was almost six thousand, while the Confederates lost several hundred more. ★

Hooker's Battle Above The Clouds, And Winning Of The Confederate Position On Lookout Mountain, November 24th, 1863.

By eight o'clock on Tuesday, November 24th, General Hooker's column was moving up Lookout Valley, and, to the surprise of the enemy, disappeared in the woods south of Wauhatchie. Then, filing his troops to the left, Hooker began the difficult task of the ascent of the mountain. The head of his column went into line of battle facing to the north, and was ordered forward, with a heavy line of skirmishers thrown out. Advancing along the slope of the ridge, the Federals took the unsuspecting enemy from the rear. As the Confederates retreated, the Federal batteries on Moccasin Point and those of the Confederates on Lookout Mountain opened a heavy fire upon each other, and soon the whole mountain was hidden from Chattanooga by the cloud of smoke which rose above and around it. With resistance stiffening, the Federals reorganized to assault the highest breastworks. Then, with one charge of the whole line, Hooker carried the position.

Capture Of Missionary Ridge, Near Rossville, By General Thomas, November 25th, 1863.

The Enthusiasm Of The Northern Armies — Reenlistment Of The Seventeenth Army Corps.

In late 1863, most of the Federal regiments agreed to reenlist when their time was up. In some corps almost all the regiments reenlisted: In the Seventeenth Army Corps thirty-nine regiments took their stand as veterans. We give artistically a view of this corps' enthusiasm. Soldiers were given several weeks of leave after reenlisting.

The War In Georgia — Stevenson, Ala., Depot For General Rosecrans's Army.

The campaign of General Rosecrans brought him to a district where it was not easy to remember the state in which places were. Chattanooga, the object of the struggle, was in Tennessee; but the battle of Chickamauga was fought in Georgia, and Rosecrans's depot of supplies was in Alabama. As a man may actually stand in three states, we may credit the assertion that from Lookout Mountain your eye can discern seven of the sovereignties of the New World. In the railroad line from Memphis, which at Cleveland, Tennessee, branches to Lynchburg, Raleigh, Charleston, Savannah, and Montgomery, Stevenson is an important point as a junction for a railroad from Nashville.

FEDERAL ARMIES PUSH INTO THE DEEP SOUTH

During the second half of 1863 the Confederates occupied Texas and carried on guerrilla warfare in Arkansas and Missouri. Some of their leaders attempted to assemble forces numbering several thousand, especially in Arkansas, but they were defeated by Union troops. Guerrilla bands, however, caused trouble for the Federals. At Lawrence, Kansas, in August a band led by Colonel William C. Quantrill committed one of the war's worst atrocities.

Quantrill's raiders dashed into this defenseless town, home to free-state abolitionists since the 1850s, and began to pillage and slaughter. One hundred and fifty men and boys were killed, and the town was burned to the ground, with charred bodies lying everywhere.

[Afterward,] the horrible scene . . . is thus described by one of the citizens: "I have read of outrages committed in the so-called dark ages, and, horrible as they appeared to me, they sink into insignificance in comparison with what I was then compelled to witness . . . Our strength failed us [and] many could not help crying like children. Women and little children were all over town, hunting for their husbands and fathers, and sad indeed was the scene when they did finally find them among the corpses laid out for recognition."

At the beginning of September, General Banks, headquartered at New Orleans, ordered General W. B. Franklin, with four thousand troops, to seize Sabine Pass, between Louisiana and Texas. Four gunboats were detached from the Gulf squadron to cooperate with Franklin, but two were disabled and captured, resulting in the expedition's failure.

Attempting to take possession of key coastal harbors, Banks dispatched six thousand troops and some vessels to the Rio Grande, and by November the expedition had fought its way to Brownsville. When the year closed, all the important positions on the Texas coast—except for Galveston Island and a fort near the mouth of the Brazos River—had fallen to the Federals. ★

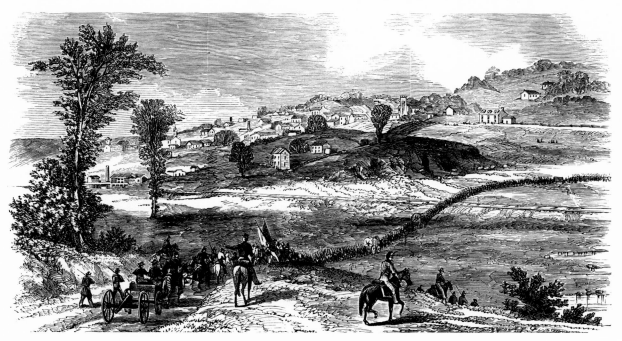

Troops Of General McPherson Entering Clinton, Miss., On Raid To Canton.

To facilitate the movements of the Federal armies near Chattanooga and divert the Confederate forces from hastening to the relief of Bragg, General James B. McPherson marched from Vicksburg on October 15th, 1863, and on the 17th came up with the enemy in a strong position ten miles beyond Brownsville. After a short, sharp fight, he routed them, the Federals charging gallantly over the bridge and through tall grass and corn to attack the enemy's line. The next day he entered Clinton, on the Vicksburg and Jackson Railroad. His troops broke the Sabbath stillness of the place as they marched in. General McPherson then proceeded to Canton, and finally returned to Vicksburg after destroying Confederate mills and factories.

Disabling And Capture Of The Federal Gunboats "Clifton" And "Sachem," In The Attack On Sabine Pass, Tex., September 8th, 1863.

One of the objects of this expedition was to take Sabine City; and on September 8th generals Franklin and G. Weitzel proceeded to the pass, prepared to enter with their troops as soon as the enemy's batteries were silenced. The only preparation for attack was to send the Clifton, an old Staten Island ferry boat, and the Sachem, *an inferior propeller-driven vessel, to attack the batteries. Carrying about one hundred sharpshooters, the vessels advanced firing, but did not elicit a reply till they were well in range, when the batteries opened. The Sachem* was soon crippled and forced to strike her colors, while a shell penetrated the boiler of the Clifton, *causing an explosion that made her a perfect wreck. Many were killed, and nearly all that survived were made prisoners.*

The War In Louisiana — Army Of General Banks Crossing Vermilion Bayou, October 10th, 1863.

As shown in our engraving, General Banks laid pontoon bridges to cross Vermilion Bayou, where the enemy had destroyed the bridge. The pontoon *bridges could be quickly removed for the next crossing.*

The War In Louisiana — General Franklin's Army Crossing The Prairie In Lafayette Parish.

The War In Mississippi — General McPherson's Army Crossing The Big Black, October 15th, 1863.

When the Confederates began to concentrate all their available forces before Rosecrans at Chattanooga, a diversion was made by General J. B. McPherson, who led an expedition into Mississippi as far as Canton. General McPherson, whom the Confederates had learned to respect at Vicksburg, moved rapidly and struck severely. Our sketch represents his army crossing the Big Black River by bridge and ford at Messenger's Ferry.

THE CONFEDERACY FIGHTS FOR ITS LIFE

It was with great satisfaction that Unionists heard the British would no longer build ships for the Confederacy, which armed them to attack United States commerce. Federal victories and Lincoln's emancipation of slaves had forced Britain to accept the legitimacy of the Union cause. Without British political support and economic ties, the Confederates were alone and facing defeat.

Leslie's described the beginning of the end for the "Great Rebellion," as Southerners called the Civil War:

The third year of the Civil War, 1864, opened encouragingly for the believers in the Union. There were many signs pointing to the early downfall of the Confederacy. More than 50,000 square miles of territory had been recovered by the Federals, and there were about 800,000 Federal troops in the field against only half that number of Confederates. The people in the Southern States were no longer willing to volunteer for the military service, and the authorities at Richmond were getting desperate. They passed a law declaring every white man in the Confederacy liable to bear arms to be in the military service, and that upon his failure to report for duty at a military station within a certain time he was liable to the penalty of death as a deserter!

In March 1864 Lincoln appointed Ulysses S. Grant as lieutenant general in command of all the Federal armies. Ordered to decisively defeat the Confederacy as soon as possible, Grant developed a direct and crushing strategy. The Army of the Potomac would strike relentlessly at Richmond, and Sherman would move swiftly on Atlanta, Georgia, the great Southern railroad center. ★

The Banks Expedition — Scene On The Levee, Baton Rouge, La. — Contrabands Unloading Military Stores From The United States Transport "North Star," Over The Mississippi Steamer "Iberville."

Upon the surrender of New Orleans, the Iberville was taken possession of by United States authorities. It was a transport during Banks's expedition, several times running the gauntlet of Confederate batteries and guerrillas. On one occasion, she sustained running fire from a battery of six guns for at least twenty minutes. Four men were killed and four wounded, one of her engines was disabled, and her upper works were riddled.

Defeat Of Confederate Cavalry By The Second Wisconsin Cavalry Near Red Bone Church, Miss.

CHAPTER 8
THE CONFEDERACY FIGHTS ON

Siege Of Charleston, S. C. — 1. Bombardment Of Fort Moultrie And Batteries Bee And Beauregard By The Monitors And "Ironsides," September 7th-8th, 1863. — 2. Interior Of Battery Gregg, Looking Toward Fort Wagner.

The bombardment of Fort Moultrie and the batteries on Sullivan's Island, on the 7th and 8th of September, was of the most determined and vigorous character, the Ironsides *devoting herself to the fort, while the monitors paid their respects to Batteries Bee and Beauregard. Our artist gives a striking sketch as viewed from a favorable point. Moultrie House is on the extreme right, next to Moultrieville, on fire, the dark smoke of the burning houses contrasting with the white puffs of smoke from the cannon thundering along the whole line. Behind* Ironsides *is Fort Moultrie; the Confederate battery to the extreme left is Battery Bee; and nearly in front of it, the second in the line of monitors, is the staunch* Weehawken, *aground.*

Bombardment of Fort Moultrie.

The Harbor Of Charleston, S. C. — Fort Moultrie, On Sullivan's Island.

THE FEDERAL CAMPAIGN to capture Charleston, South Carolina, began in the spring of 1863 and continued throughout the war. As the original flashpoint of the rebellion, Charleston was targeted for capture by the Federal government to prove its superiority over the Confederacy. The harbor's most formidable barrier was Fort Sumter, which along with other shore batteries repulsed a springtime naval expedition commanded by Admiral S. F. du Pont.

That summer General Quincy A. Gillmore took command of another expedition against Charleston, planning first to seize Fort Wagner, on Morris Island, and use its guns in silencing Fort Sumter. The expedition's naval vessels were commanded by Admiral John A. Dahlgren. On July 10 Gillmore landed troops on Morris Island and the next day attacked Fort Wagner but was unsuccessful. On July 18 Dahlgren's fleet and Federal land batteries began bombarding Wagner, and at sunset assault troops moved in two columns to attack. One column was led by General George C. Strong, the other by Colonel H. L. Putnam. Strong's brigade was composed of the Fifty-fourth Massachusetts (Colored) Regiment, under Colonel R. G. Shaw, and the Sixth Connecticut, Forty-eighth New York, Third New Hampshire, Seventy-sixth Pennsylvania, and Ninth Maine.

Rushing forward, the troops were overwhelmed by a storm of shot and shell from the fort and other Confederate positions, including Sumter. The attackers pressed onward, and the fire from the garrison was so hot that all but one of six regimental commanders was hit and Strong was wounded. As the Fifty-fourth reached Wagner's parapet, Colonel Shaw fell dead. Under heavy fire, the troops tried to hold their positions outside the walls, but the defenders had every advantage, and the Federals were forced to retreat.

Colonel Putnam's brigade next attacked through that storm of fire, gaining the ramparts, and in fierce hand-to-hand fighting entered part of the fort. Putnam attempted to maintain a foothold until reinforcements arrived, but he was mortally wounded, and his exhausted men had to retreat. Fort Wagner had held out.

Some days after the assault, General Strong also died. Of the more than fifty-two hundred Union troops engaged, more than fifteen hundred were casualties; the Confederates lost one hundred seventy-four men out of almost eighteen hundred defenders. ★

CHARLESTON UNDER SIEGE

In July of 1863, General Gillmore began a siege of Fort Wagner and ordered a battery to be built in a swamp within range of Morris Island. He called for driving piles into deep mud and building a firing platform upon them.

When Gillmore ordered a lieutenant of engineers to attend to the construction of this battery the latter told him such a thing would be impossible. "There is no such word as impossible," said Gillmore. "Call for what you need." The lieutenant at once made a requisition on the quartermaster for "one hundred men eighteen feet high to wade in mud sixteen feet deep." But although this requisition could not be honored the redoubt was built by bringing timber for the piles . . . in rafts.

After two weeks the platform was mounted with seven cannon. The heaviest gun, called the "Swamp Angel" had a range of almost five miles, reaching Charleston. One shell struck St. Michael's Church and destroyed a tablet containing the Ten Commandments. Still legible was the commandment "Thou shalt not kill."

On August 17 the Federal fleet and batteries began a constant bombardment of Fort Sumter, while troops were digging trenches nearer and nearer to Fort Wagner. On September 6 they came close enough to reach the ramparts in one short assault. That night, the Confederates fled rather than wait for the attack. Morris Island's guns were now directed against Fort Sumter, and the steady bombardments destroyed all the fort's artillery. On the night of September 8 four hundred troops went in small boats to take possession of Sumter, but the garrison drove them back with great loss. Sumter would not be abandoned. ★

The "Grand Skedaddle" Of The Inhabitants From Charleston, S. C., When Threatened By An Attack; Sketched From The Federal Prison.

As Federal forces moved against Charleston, the terror among the civilians was very great. Despite the fact that General Beauregard with thirty thousand troops was stationed midway between Charleston and Savannah, a restless desire for flight took possession of thousands, and for three days the roads to the interior were crowded with as miscellaneous a group as that which marched into Noah's Ark. Lieutenant Kirby, of the Forty-seventh Massachusetts Regiment, being then a prisoner, had an excellent opportunity of sketching this motley stream of humanity.

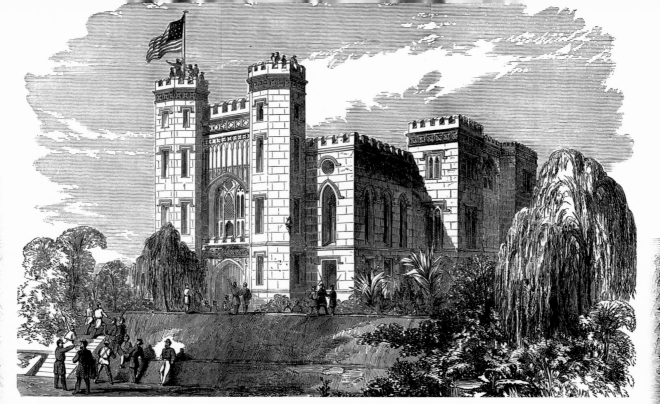

The Siege Of Charleston — Ordnance Depot, Morris Island, S. C.

A CITY IN RUINS

After silencing Fort Sumter's guns, the Federals did not immediately attempt the capture of Charleston but gradually destroyed this once-thriving seaport by bombardment and siege. There was a lack of food, and many residents fled inland for safety.

A picture of the desolate city under siege was given in a Southern newspaper, quoted by *Leslie's*:

Here and there, a pedestrian moves hurriedly along, and the rattle of a cart or a dray is alone heard for a whole square. The blinds are closed; vases of rare exotics droop and wither on the lonely window sill, because there is no tender hand to twine or nourish them. The walk glistens with fragments of glass, rattled thither by the concussion of exploding shells; here a cornice is knocked off; there, is a small round hole through the side of a building; beyond, a house in ruins, and at remote intervals the earth is torn where a shell exploded, and looks like the work of a giant in search of some hidden treasure; and little tufts of bright-green grass are springing up along the pave, once vocal with the myriad tongues of busy trade.

Yet Charleston's defenders stubbornly held on. Much of the time they were directed by the able General P.G.T. Beauregard, now commander of the coastal defenses of the Carolinas and Georgia. ★

Loading A Fifteen-inch Gun In The Turret Of An Ironclad During The Attack On Fort Sumter.

The Ironclad "Weehawken" Returning To Fire A Parting Shot At Fort Sumter, After The Bombardment That Failed To Silence The Fort, April 7th, 1863.

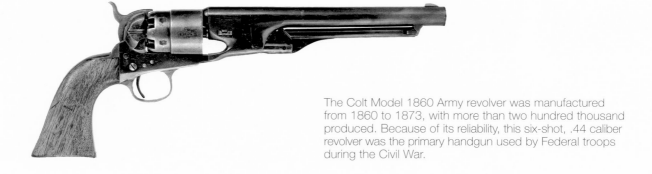

The Colt Model 1860 Army revolver was manufactured from 1860 to 1873, with more than two hundred thousand produced. Because of its reliability, this six-shot, .44 caliber revolver was the primary handgun used by Federal troops during the Civil War.

Siege Of Charleston — The Doomed City Fired By Shells From Fort Putnam, January 3d, 1864.

Federal Sharpshooters Approaching Fort Wagner Before The Confederates Evacuated.

SHARPSHOOTERS

The First Regiment of U.S. Sharpshooters was better known as Berdan's Sharpshooters, named for its commander, Colonel Hiram Berdan. At the start of the war, Berdan, a New Yorker, was considered the finest rifle shot in the country. He was promoted to major general after the Gettysburg campaign, where his men played a key role in the victory. The Second Regiment of sharpshooters was commanded by Colonel Henry A. Post. Deadly accurate with the Sharps .52 caliber rifle, these marksmen were lethal at three hundred yards and could hit a target at six hundred yards. (The term "sharpshooter" has nothing to do with the Sharps rifle they used.) Dressed in green, sharpshooters generally served as skirmishers on the perimeter of the army in the field. It is estimated the Second Regiment slew more men than any other regiment in the army. For all their effectiveness, sharpshooters—snipers, who killed from a distance, unseen and unexpected—were often despised, considered cold-blooded killers by the average soldiers on both sides who were their targets.

Berdan's
Sharpshooters
Uniform

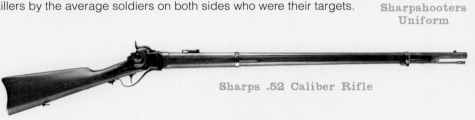

Sharps .52 Caliber Rifle

THE CAVALRY ARM GROWS STRONGER

During the Civil War the cavalry operated as scouts and raiders for the most part, and pitched battles between major bodies of mounted troops were rare. One of the most important cavalry engagements was also the first: Brandy Station, Virginia, also known as Beverly Ford. The start to the Gettysburg campaign of June 1863, this daylong series of charges and countercharges cost the Federals more than nine hundred casualties, the Confederates more than five hundred. The engagement revealed to the Federals that Lee's army was moving north, and it also proved that Northern cavalry could fight on equal terms with the Southerners. The famed Confederate cavalry general J. E. B. Stuart was deeply embarrassed that the Federal attack at Brandy Station had taken him by surprise.

Rush's Lancers Guarding The Roads In Maryland, To Prevent The Passage Of Civilians Who Would Be Caught Up In A Battle.

Desperate Hand-to-hand Combat Between Federal Cavalry, Commanded By General Averell, And Stuart's Confederate Troops, At Kelly's Ford, On The Rappahannock, Va., March 17th, 1863.

One of the first stand-up cavalry fights took place at Kelly's Ford, on the Rappahannock, in early 1863. To the Federal general W. W. Averell and the Confederate general Fitzhugh Lee belong the chief honors of this affair. General Averell's command took on the *Confederate forces under generals Stuart and Fitz Lee. The Confederates, made desperate by the advance of Federal troops across the Rappahannock and upon the soil which they had sworn to defend with the last drop of their blood, disputed every rood of ground. Again* *and again they charged on the Federal lines, and as often were they repulsed in the most gallant manner. The object of the reconnaissance expedition having been accomplished, General Averell retired across the river without molestation from the enemy.*

Gallant Charge Of The Sixth Michigan Cavalry Over The Enemy's Breastworks, Near Falling Waters, Md., July 14th, 1863.

The exploits of the Federal cavalry in Virginia, Maryland, and Pennsylvania in 1863 would fill a volume in themselves. Among the many gallant charges there are few more brilliant than that of the Sixth Michigan at Falling Waters, where they rode, without drawing rein, right over the Confederate breastworks, scattering all before. The cavalry were not more than sixty at most, but they charged up a steep hill in the face of a terrific fire; and though they lost in killed and wounded nearly two-thirds of their number, they captured almost the entire force of the enemy, with three regimental battle flags.

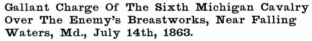

One of the most famous and successful Union cavalry commanders of the war was General Phillip H. Sheridan, who carried this saber. The scabbard is engraved with the names of Sheridan's battles, which included Five Forks, Stones River, Chickamauga, and Chattanooga.

The War In Louisiana — The Advance On Shreveport, Crossing Cane River, March 31st, 1864.

The Army of the Gulf, under General Franklin, crosses the Cane River by bridges and pontoons at a point fifty-four miles from Alexandria. The expedition failed, and commanding general Banks was replaced.

THE RED RIVER CAMPAIGN OF 1864

General Nathaniel Banks organized another invasion into Texas along the Red River early in 1864, cooperating with Admiral Porter's fleet of thirteen ironclads and seven light-draft gunboats. A detachment from Sherman's army also participated, operating independently for the most part.

Banks reached Sabine Cross Roads, where nine thousand Confederates under General Richard Taylor made a stand, defeating the Federals on April 8. Banks retreated, was pursued, and the next day another battle was fought at Pleasant Hill. This time Banks repulsed Taylor, but the expedition still had to fall back to Grand Ecore on the Red River. There, Porter's larger vessels were unable to proceed because the waters were too shallow. The river was falling rapidly, and the fleet had difficulty in passing the sandbars—even to withdraw.

Banks intended to return to the Mississippi River, but the fleet was almost grounded. The Confederates harassed exposed Federal positions and destroyed five gunboats, threatening the entire fleet. The situation was desperate.

The water in the rapids of the Red River at Alexandria had become so shallow that to get the fleet past them the river above had to be dammed and the vessels floated down over the rocks on the bosom of the flood that was suddenly set free through sluices. This was done with great skill and industry under the direction of Lieutenant Colonel Joseph Bailey, of a Wisconsin regiment.

Bailey was a trained engineer in charge of the defenses of New Orleans, where Banks now returned, soon to be replaced as a field commander.

The failure of this expedition led Sterling Price to plan another Confederate invasion of Missouri in September with twenty thousand men. Hoping to win recruits, Price got halfway to St. Louis but was defeated, and his army shattered. ★

General Edward R. S. Canby.

General Canby, born in Kentucky in 1819, graduated West Point in 1839 and served in the Florida and Mexican wars. As acting brigadier general in New Mexico in 1862 he repelled Confederate general and fellow West Pointer H. H. Sibley in his attempt to acquire possession of that territory. In the spring of 1864, Canby replaced Banks as field commander in the Mississippi-Texas theater.

Capture Of Fort De Russy, La., On March 14th, 1864, By Forces Under General A. J. Smith.

This expedition left Vicksburg on March 10th, landed at Summerville, La., on the 13th, and marched with little opposition to Fort de Russy. At four o'clock in the afternoon the Third and Ninth Indiana batteries opened on the fort, which replied vigorously with three of its heaviest guns. The cannonade continued an hour, when General Smith ordered his troops to storm the fort. Within twenty minutes after the order was given the color sergeant of the Fifty-eighth Illinois Volunteers planted the American flag upon the enemy's works.

Battle Of Resaca, Ga., May 14th, 1864 — General J. W. Geary's Brigade Charging Up The Mountain.

A Federal Wagon Train Passes Resaca As Sherman Maneuvers Around Johnston's Defenses.

SHERMAN MOVES AGAINST ATLANTA

General W.T. Sherman, who took charge in the western theater in the spring of 1864 when Grant left to assume the post of lieutenant general over all the Federal armies, began his campaign against Atlanta, the South's main railroad hub, on May 6.

Leading one hundred thousand men, Sherman first outflanked a force of sixty thousand at Dalton, Georgia, commanded by General Joseph E. Johnston. Sherman's maneuver forced Johnston's retreat to Resaca Station, and after a sharp fight on May 15, Johnston withdrew through strategic Allatoona Pass and took up a strong defensive position.

Severe fighting continued until June 1, when Johnston was again compelled to withdraw. Sherman pushed on, contested by Johnston wherever a stand could be made. After a month of desperate fighting, the Confederates were driven from the Kenesaw Mountains toward Atlanta.

When Johnston reached the Chattahoochee Sherman . . . at once planned to strike a severe blow on his antagonist while he was crossing that river. But Johnston was too quick and skillful to allow this, and he safely passed the stream and made a stand along the line of it. He was soon forced from this position and retreated to a new line that covered Atlanta, his left resting on the Chattahoochee and his right on Peachtree Creek.

On July 10, Johnston was succeeded by General J.B. Hood, of Texas. On July 20, Hood led the next counterattack but was repulsed. Now Sherman moved rapidly toward Atlanta, fighting off furious counterstrokes and driving the Confederates back to their works. Sherman was victorious, but leading Union general James B. McPherson was killed by a sharpshooter.

On August 31 Hood was defeated at Jonesborough, in the decisive battle for Atlanta. Hood recrossed the Chattahoochee, and Sherman entered Atlanta on September 2.★

The Campaign In Georgia — Federal Troops Foraging Near Warsaw Sound.

Sherman's Campaign In Georgia — The Attack On Kenesaw Mountain, June 22d, 1864.

Kenesaw Mountain, a second Lookout among its fellows, is about four miles in length and some four hundred feet high, difficult of ascent, with spurs on the flanks. Sherman resolved to flank it, and on June 22nd the corps of the right and left of his army advanced, the center maintaining its position around and upon the base of the mountain in the teeth of a very heavy artillery fire from the Confederate batteries. The Twentieth and Twenty-third wheeled on the left to hem in the Confederates between the Federal line and the railroad. The enemy counterattacked furiously to check the movement, but Schofield and Hooker were ready, and the enemy was driven back with artillery alone. Again, about six o'clock, the Confederates made the same attempt and were driven back by a combined, destructive fire of artillery and musketry. The next Federal objective would be the city of Atlanta.

The Federal Capture Of Lost Mountain By General Hooker, June 16th, 1864.

General Hooker pushed forward, with General J. W. Geary's troops in the advance. Hooker's lines drove the enemy's pickets rapidly before them, halting now and then to dislodge some of the more stubborn of the Confederates, who maintained their fire until almost under the feet of the advancing troops. A fierce struggle lasted until after dark. The morning of the 15th opened with heavy firing, to repel an attack of the Confederates. Artillery was placed along the lines and took a prominent part in the struggle, which continued with varying intensity till after nightfall. Early on the morning of the 16th Geary's skirmishers discovered the enemy had evacuated, and they immediately pushed into the works. Sherman soon pushed on to attack Johnston at Kenesaw Mountain.

MARCH TO THE SEA

Sherman started for the Georgia coast on November 14, with sixty thousand men arranged in two wings and led by five thousand cavalry.

They marched for more than a month through the heart of Georgia, living entirely upon what they picked up on the way. Moving as they did in two columns, with wings extending sixty miles, the Confederates were bewildered, and offered but very little opposition.

Meanwhile, General Thomas was operating against Hood, who pushed toward Nashville with fifty thousand men. Hood drove Federal troops from Franklin on November 30 and laid siege to Nashville, where Thomas arrived to take command. By December 15 Thomas had counterattacked, and the defeated Hood retreated southward.

On December 21, Sherman entered the port city of Savannah, Georgia, which had just been evacuated by the Confederates. ★

Sherman's Campaign In Georgia — Federal Forces At Jonesborough, Destroying The Macon Railroad.

The Siege Of Atlanta, Ga. — Confederate Attack On General J. A. Logan's Corps, July 28th, 1864.

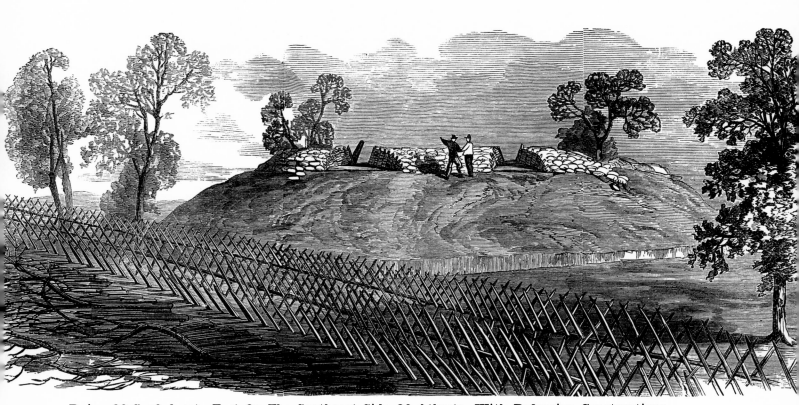

Ruins Of Confederate Fort On The Southeast Side Of Atlanta, With Defensive Constructions, Chevaux-de-frise And Abatis, Still Remaining Standing In Front.

CHAPTER 9
GRANT'S RELENTLESS ASSAULTS

Presentation Of Colors To The Twentieth United States Colored Infantry In New York City.

The Twentieth Regiment, United States Colored Troops, left Riker's Island at nine o'clock on the 5th of March, 1864, on board the steamer John Romer, *and was conveyed to the foot of Twenty-first Street, East River, New York, where they were disembarked and formed in regimental line, and marched to Union Square, arriving in front of the Union League Clubhouse at one o'clock. A vast crowd of citizens, of every shade of color and every phase of social and political life, filled the square and streets, and every door, window, veranda, tree and housetop that commanded a view of the scene was peopled with spectators. Over the entrance of the clubhouse was a large platform, ornamented with flags and filled with ladies. In the street was another platform, tastefully decorated and occupied by prominent citizens. From the stand the colors were presented by President King of Columbia College, who addressed them with warmth and eloquence. After the presentation ceremony was over the men stacked arms and partook of a collation provided for them.*

THE AFRICAN AMERICAN population offered Federal forces an enormous pool from which to draw volunteers. The first black units to fight for the Union were termed "Native Guards," men mostly from the lower Mississippi and along the Carolina coast. Many were freemen, and some had been members of all-black Southern militia organizations before the war.

Early in 1863, Lincoln called for four "Negro," or "Colored," regiments, but by the end of the war there would be 166 black regiments, eventually totaling three hundred thousand men. Most were led by white officers until late in the war, when blacks were commissioned. Black volunteers helped swing the balance of the war to the North's favor.

Another key factor favoring the North was the development of an effective Federal cavalry arm. Grant's Virginia campaign involved thousands of cavalrymen, many of them serving with General Philip Sheridan in the Shenandoah Valley. One notable mounted campaign was led by General Hugh J. Kilpatrick, whose five thousand troopers raided toward Richmond in February 1864, striking at the city's defenses.

Cavalry led the Army of the Potomac on May 4, 1864, as it began a grand movement toward Richmond, advancing into the dense woods known as the Wilderness. The army was slowed by its immense train of more than four thousand wagons. The Wilderness extended from Chancellorsville to Mine Run, where Lee's army was entrenched. Lee decided to attack while Grant was passing through this wooded country and was waiting for his supply train to catch up.

On May 5 the Battle of the Wilderness began, a hard-fought conflict through thick woods of pine, cedar, scrub oak, and tangled underbrush and vines. Artillery was almost entirely useless, and although nearly two hundred thousand men were engaged in the campaign, it was difficult to see more than a thousand troops at any one time. The contest raged through the Wilderness for two days, with only darkness putting an end to the struggle and slaughter.

On the third night, after Lee did not attack that day, Grant moved to cut off his retreat and made a rapid march toward Spotsylvania Court House. ★

The War In Virginia — Sketch On The Line Of The Second Corps At The Battle Of The Wilderness, May 6th, 1864 — Waiting For The Enemy To Appear Before Them.

On the night succeeding the Federal passage of the Rapidan both armies camped nearby each other, Grant unsuspicious of the close presence of the enemy. Next day Confederate general R. S. Ewell attacked G. K. Warren's troops moving through the wood roads. Grant and Meade, at Old Wilderness Tavern, supposed this to be simply the attack of a rear guard. Before Sedgwick could come up, Ewell had inflicted a loss of three thousand men. Grant being ready to accept battle here, Sedgwick was ordered to join Warren's right, and W. S. Hancock was summoned from Chancellorsville. Both Grant and Lee determined to attack on the morrow. Burnside was ordered up to take position between Warren and Hancock. Lee awaited the arrival of Longstreet, whom he wanted to place opposite Hancock's right. Grant ordered an attack along the whole line at 5 A. M. Lee determined to turn Grant's left and throw him back upon the river. Hancock fell upon the enemy at five o'clock, and drove them back over a mile down the Plank Road. Hancock stopped to reorganize, and while thus pausing, Longstreet came upon the field and attacked him.

Hancock, by the suddenness of this attack, was driven back to his old lines on the Brock Road. Here he rallied his men, and Longstreet being wounded, the violence of the Confederate attack subsided. In the afternoon Lee again attacked Hancock; night once more intervened; nothing had been decided. Grant lost fifteen thousand men; Lee's loss was less by several thousand. Our sketch was taken on the line of the Second Corps, on the 6th, showing the gallant men of that corps awaiting the enemy's attack.

An Incident From The Battle Of The
Wilderness — Lieutenant General Grant
And Major General Meade In Consultation.

Grant's Campaign In Virginia — The Battle Of Bethesda Church, Between S. W. Crawford's Division, Fifth Corps, And The Confederates, May 30th, 1864.

Battle Of Spotsylvania Courthouse — Opening Of The Fight At Alsop's Farm, May 8th, 1864.

The direct route to Spotsylvania Courthouse is by the Brock Road, via Todd's Tavern. On this road the Fifth Corps, under General Warren, was to take the advance, and by rapid march seize Spotsylvania Courthouse. Hancock's corps was to follow on the same line, while Sedgwick and Burnside were to move on an exterior route by way of Chancellorsville. The vital interest of this movement centered in the march of Warren to seize Spotsylvania Courthouse. Warren's corps advanced at 9 P.M. on the 7th. Reaching Todd's Tavern, he was delayed for an hour and a half by the cavalry escort of General Meade blocking the way. On the 8th he was again detained, this time by the cavalry division that had been engaged in fighting and driving Stuart's cavalry, whom Lee had sent to block the Brock Road, and who still barred further advance. The cavalry, after two hours of ineffectual effort, gave way to Warren, who advanced to clear his own path. The advance brigades were deployed in line of battle, while the remainder of the corps followed in column. At 8 A.M. of the 8th the column emerged from the woods into a clearing, known as Alsop's Farm, two miles north of Spotsylvania Courthouse. Longstreet's corps had in the meantime arrived at the same place, and a sharp engagement ensued until the woods on both flanks of the Federals were cleared of the enemy. Warren waited for Sedgwick to come up. Before the latter arrived night had fallen. As a consequence of all those incidents, Lee had managed to place himself across Grant's path, and having drawn upon the Spotsylvania Ridge a bulwark of defense, he was able to hold the Army of the Potomac in check. Our illustration shows the opening of the battle of the 8th, as viewed from General Warren's headquarters.

GRANT BATTLES LEE ON THE ROAD TOWARD RICHMOND

Hearing of Grant's movement, Lee dispatched Longstreet to meet the Federal advance, and there was a race to Spotsylvania between the two opposing columns. Longstreet, knowing the country well, reached Spotsylvania first. As if continuing the battle of the Wilderness, fighting resumed as the Federals pressed toward Spotsylvania Court House. There were grave losses on both sides.

> On May 9th, General Sedgwick . . . went forward to superintend the placing of some batteries. While doing so a bullet whistled past him. He laughed and called out to the nearest enemy in sight: "Pooh, man, you can't hit an elephant at that distance!" The next moment a bullet from a sharpshooter hidden in a near-by tree entered his brain, and one of the best of generals fell dead.

While the armies were engaged in an ever more savage battle, Sheridan took his cavalry on a raid to sever Lee's communications with Richmond. Sheridan spread destruction in the rear of the Confederates, tearing up railroads and briefly reaching the outer defenses around Richmond.

At Spotsylvania the Union troops attacked again and again. On May 10, after pouring shot and shell into the Confederate positions, Grant ordered a grand assault. With cheers and shouts the columns advanced through brutal fire that swept their ranks, inflicting fearful losses, but without any gain. The engagement at Spotsylvania ended as before, with Lee withdrawing behind a new line of entrenchments. In two weeks of campaigning, the Army of the Potomac had lost nearly forty thousand men, killed, wounded, or captured, while it is estimated that Lee lost about thirty thousand.

To the southeast other battles raged, where General Butler attempted to move his twenty-five thousand men from Fortress Monroe toward Richmond, to cooperate with the Army of the Potomac. Butler soon found himself engaged with General P. G. T. Beauregard, summoned from Charleston to Richmond. By May 16 Butler's forces had been driven back to the safety of their entrenchments. ★

The War In Virginia — Sheridan's Great Battle With J. E. B. Stuart At Yellow Tavern, May 11th, 1864 — The Famed Confederate Cavalry Commander's Last Fight.

We give a sketch, which our readers cannot fail to admire, of the battle of Yellow Tavern, May 11th, 1864, where General Stuart, whose fame began by a successful raid around McClellan, fell mortally wounded. Our correspondent wrote: "We found the enemy very strongly entrenched behind fortifications composing the outer line of the Richmond defenses. The position was a strong one, being situated upon a hill, commanding our whole corps, and our preservation depended on our driving them out. General Sheridan was equal to the emergency. The enemy was already pursuing us closely in the rear. The general ordered Custer to take his gallant brigade and carry the position. General Custer placed himself at the head of his command, and with drawn sabres and deafening cheers charged directly in the face of a withering fire, captured two pieces of artillery, upward of one hundred prisoners, together with caissons, ammunition and horses, which he brought off in safety. It was, without exception, the most gallant charge of the raid." In a desperate charge at the head of a column the Confederate general Stuart fell mortally wounded.

WARFARE RETURNS TO BLOODY GROUND

As the armies of Grant and Lee battled on, in their race for Richmond, fast-moving cavalry forces clashed around them. On May 11 the brilliant Confederate cavalry leader, J. E. B. Stuart was killed by Union cavalry at Yellow Tavern.

On May 21, Grant again started his army forward, crossing the North Anna River. Lee was already there, but after the Battle of North Anna he was dislodged. Grant pressed forward, and by May 28 he was south of the Pamunkey River. Lee, however, had taken a shorter route and occupied a strong position on the Chickahominy River. Grant attempted to cross the Chickahominy at Cold Harbor.

> For three days [June 1–3] the two armies fiercely struggled on the ground where Lee and McClellan had fought two years before. The battle on the 3d was particularly sanguinary, thousands of men falling in the brief space of twenty minutes. At its conclusion the Federals . . . had failed in their attempt to force the Chickahominy. The strength of Lee's position showed Grant that Richmond could not be taken in that direction.

Grant decided to transfer his army to the south side of the James River and approach the Confederate capital from that way. On the night of June 12 his army silently withdrew, crossing the Chickahominy at Long Bridge. Grant next moved to the James, which he crossed in boats and on pontoon bridges.

> Grant hurried on . . . while the crossing was being made and ordered Butler to send a portion of his troops to attempt the capture of Petersburg before Lee could re-enforce Beauregard. But this was unsuccessful, and on the evening of June 16th the Army of the Potomac took up a position near a strong line of intrenchments that Beauregard had cast up around the city.

At this time General Jubal Early, with about fifteen thousand Confederate troops, marched from the Shenandoah Valley, through Maryland, and threatened Washington itself. Early discovered at the last moment that Washington's fortifications were too strong and too well mounted with artillery to assault, and he withdrew. ★

The War In Virginia — General Butler's Lines South Of The James, With Troops In Position, Awaiting An Attack Prior To The Arrival Of General Grant's Army, June 3d, 1864.

The sudden transfer of operations by General Grant from the old battle-ground on the Chickahominy, historic from the bloody campaign of 1862, and laden with deadly miasma of the Chickahominy swamps, to the point south of the James River occupied by General B. F. Butler, gave that comparatively fresh locality additional interest to the public. We lay before our readers a sketch of the fortifications between the James and the Appomattox. Our view is taken from within, showing the shelter in the tents inside the works, and the men manning the line, awaiting an attack of the enemy. Lee, however, remained on the defensive around Richmond and Petersburg.

Remains Of A Confederate Camp At Manassas.

The Operations Near Washington — Scene Of The Fight At Fort Stevens, July 12th–13th, 1864.

When news of General Early's invasion reached Grant he sent up to City Point the old Sixth Corps, whence they embarked for Washington. They went perhaps enjoying the scare of the Washington people, little suspecting that they were to have a brilliant little battle of their own under the eyes of the President. About six o'clock on the 12th the Confederates showed themselves coming down a declivity on both sides of Seventh Street road (Brookville Turnpike) into a little valley running across the road about a mile north of Fort Stevens. A brigade of infantry was ordered to clear out the enemy. The dwellings on the hill opposite, shelters for sharpshooters, were preliminarily emptied by shells, which set them on fire — shells sent from Forts Massachusetts and Slocum. Then the Federal infantry rose, and, with a fanlike spreading to the right and left, dashed with hurrahs of delight at the two positions on each side of the Seventh Street road. The Confederates retreated, and a regiment of their cavalry issued from a wood, to the succor of their flying infantry and sharpshooters. The Federals halted to receive the troopers' charge, fired into them at close quarters, checked them, fired again, and kept firing. In three minutes neither Confederate cavalry nor infantry was in sight. The Federals double-quicked in line of battle over the crest of the heights, and disappeared in pursuit, with hurrahs and laughter, on the other side, driving two divisions of Ewell's corps in headlong flight before them.

The War In Virginia — The Eighteenth Army Corps Storming A Fort On The Right Of The Confederate Line Before Petersburg, June 15th, 1864.

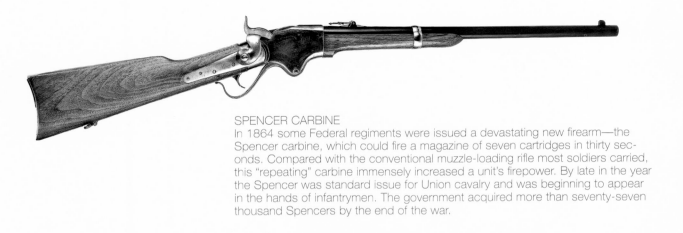

SPENCER CARBINE
In 1864 some Federal regiments were issued a devastating new firearm—the Spencer carbine, which could fire a magazine of seven cartridges in thirty seconds. Compared with the conventional muzzle-loading rifle most soldiers carried, this "repeating" carbine immensely increased a unit's firepower. By late in the year the Spencer was standard issue for Union cavalry and was beginning to appear in the hands of infantrymen. The government acquired more than seventy-seven thousand Spencers by the end of the war.

SHERIDAN'S RIDE TO SAVE THE DAY

Early moved his force back into the Shenandoah Valley, where he engaged in a series of battles with Federal troops under the command of General Sheridan.

Sheridan defeated Early at Winchester on September 19 and at Fisher's Hill three days later. Early returned in a few weeks and attacked Sheridan's unsuspecting troops at Cedar Creek, driving them back.

General Sheridan was at Winchester when the attack began, and hearing the sound of the guns, sprang upon his black charger and dashed toward Cedar Creek. Meeting on the way portions of his army in confused retreat, he galloped up to them, and waving his hat shouted: "Face the other way, boys—face the other way! We are going back to our camp to lick them out of their boots!" Instantly the tide was turned, and following their commander, the troops hurriedly retraced their steps toward the lost battle ground.

Early's force was almost annihilated, putting an end to hostilities in the Shenandoah Valley.

Grant and Lee continued their own confrontation, with Richmond as the Federal objective. Petersburg, stoutly defended, was under siege, and neither army could get the upper hand that summer. ★

Artillery Battery Of The Third Division, Ninth Army Corps, Shelling Petersburg.

Our readers will be able to study the siege of Petersburg in our illustrations as they did that of Vicksburg. It is one of those cases where pictorial illustra- tion has an advantage over mere verbal accounts. Here we see the Thirty-fourth New York Battery and the Seventh Maine of the Third Division of Burnside's Ninth Army Corps, shelling the city of Petersburg itself as it stands in full sight, less than three miles off.

WAR ON THE WATERS

Although the Confederacy did not build a seagoing fleet to oppose the U.S. Navy, its fast cruisers, purchased from and built in Britain, made great havoc among the merchant ships of the Union. By the beginning of 1864 they had captured 193 vessels, whose aggregate cargoes were valued at $13.4 million. Most Southern coastal cities were blockaded throughout the war. One of the key victories for the U.S. Navy was the August 1864 attack by Admiral David Farragut's fleet on the harbor defenses of Mobile, Alabama. At one point Farragut commanded while lashed to the rigging to avoid falling if wounded. This was one of the last major Confederate ports to be captured.

Farragut's Naval Victory In Mobile Harbor — His Flagship, The "Hartford," Engaging The Confederate Ram "Tennessee," Which Was Finally Defeated And Captured By Union Ironclads.

Floating Mines — Infernal Machine Designed By The Confederates To Destroy The Federal Flotilla In The Potomac Discovered By Captain Budd Of The Steamer "Resolute."

Floating mines designed by the Confederates to blow up the vessels of the Potomac flotilla were intercepted on July 7, 1861. The following description was sent to the Navy Department: "Two large eighty-eight gallon oil casks, perfectly watertight, acting as buoys, connected by twenty-five fathoms of three-and-a-half-inch rope, buoyed with large squares of cork, every two feet secured to casks by iron handles. A heavy bomb of boiler iron, fitted with a brass tap and filled with powder, was suspended to the casks six feet under water. On top of the casks was a wooden box, with fuse in a gutta-percha tube. In the center of the cork was a platform with a great length of fuse coiled away, occupying the middle of the cask."

Capture Of The Anglo-Confederate Steamer "Aries" Off Bull's Bay, Near Charleston, S. C., By The United States Gunboat "Stettin."

Siege Of Petersburg — The Ninth Corps Charging On The Enemy's Works After The Explosion Of The Mine, July 30th, 1864. The Union Attack Was Bloodily Repulsed.

STALEMATE AND SIEGE

While the Army of the Potomac entrenched before Petersburg in the summer of 1864, Lee withdrew a large force from that city to counter troops sent by Butler toward Richmond.

Grant took advantage of this, and made several attempts to penetrate the Confederate lines before Petersburg. He succeeded in undermining one of the principal forts, and on the morning of July 30th the whole fort, with 300 men, was blown high into the air. Then a heavy cannonade was opened . . . with great effect. But the assault was a failure, owing to slowness of motion of some of the assailants.

The Confederates swiftly recovered from the explosion and poured destructive fire on the attackers, trapping many in the deep crater formed by the blast. Federal commanders, including General Burnside, failed to exploit the Petersburg Mine Assault, or "Battle of the Crater," as the engagement was also called. It was a "stupendous failure," according to Grant, who lost nearly thirty-eight hundred men, compared with about fifteen hundred Confederates. Many of the assault troops were from black regiments.

In December, Federal troops massed south of the James and attacked Lee's works on Hatcher's Run but were repulsed. Grant withdrew to his entrenchments in front of Petersburg, and very little more was done until the opening of the 1865 campaign.

Meanwhile, Lincoln had been reelected president that fall in a resounding victory over the Democrats' candidate, George B. McClellan. With Lincoln as the North's leader, there would be no negotiating for peace. The government would fight to win an unconditional victory and unify the nation again. ★

Charge Of The Second Division, Ninth Army Corps, Into The Crater, July 30th, 1864.

The charge made by the Second Division of the Ninth Army Corps is shown from the hand of one who witnessed it nearby. It was made bravely, but from faults which could not be explained valuable time had been lost, officers were absent, and the result was a sad slaughter of men which the country could not afford *to lose. On arriving at the exploded fort the Federals found it a heterogeneous mass of loose earth, guns and gun carriages, dead and wounded gunners, etc. One of the charging officers, noticing the earth move near him as if a mole or gopher were at work under it, commenced digging, and finally extricated* *a Confederate lieutenant, who actually revived and conversed freely with the officer before being brought from the ground. Several others were exhumed from their living graves and restored to consciousness. The tunnel was dug by coal miners directed by an officer who was a mining engineer.*

The War In Virginia — Burnside's Corps Charging The Confederate Position On The Right Of The Enemy's Line In Front Of Petersburg.

The War In Virginia — The Twenty-second Colored Regiment Carrying The First Line Of Confederate Works Before Petersburg In Grant's Campaign Of 1864.

The Siege Of Petersburg — The Fifth Corps Awaiting The Order To Advance, July 30th, 1864.

Siege Of Petersburg — Colored Infantry Bringing In Captured Guns Amid Cheers Of Ohio Troops.

PEACE UNDER ONLY ONE FLAG

The Civil War was coming to an end. Several efforts had been made by various individuals to bring about peace without the need to conquer the Confederacy by force of arms, but these had failed.

President Lincoln would listen to no conditions except absolute submission, everywhere within the bounds of the republic, to the National authority, and the entire abolition of slavery. When Jefferson Davis, in answer to an appeal from Francis P. Blair, of Maryland, near the close of the year 1864, said that he would be willing to "enter into a conference with a view to secure peace to the two countries," President Lincoln expressed his willingness to confer if it was with a view "to secure peace for the people of our common country."

Davis appointed a commission for discussions, but the conference was fruitless, because Lincoln would not waver from his position. At a Richmond public meeting on February 5, 1865, Davis declared,

"Sooner than we should be united again, I would be willing to yield up everything I have on earth and, if it were possible, would sacrifice my life a thousand times before I would succumb." Then a few days later at another meeting it was resolved that the Confederates would never lay down their arms until their independence was won. ★

The Siege Of Petersburg — Battle Of Ream's Station — The Attempt Of The Enemy To Regain The Weldon Railroad On The Evening Of August 25th, 1864.

The enemy having been repulsed, the Federal skirmishers followed, advancing nearly to the position they had formerly held, and capturing a number of prisoners. Shortly after the enemy again advanced, and were again driven back with heavy loss; and their third assault, made about 4 P. M., was attended with a like satisfactory result. In the first three charges the enemy used no artillery, but about 4 P. M. they opened a heavy, concentrated fire from a number of batteries, pouring a storm of shell and other missiles over the entire amphitheater included within the Federal lines. After about twenty minutes of this artillery fire the enemy again made their appearance. Emerging from the woods, they advanced in two lines of battle. The Federal artillery and musketry greeted them, as before, with a rapid fire, but without checking their progress. On they came, with bayonets fixed and without firing a shot. They approached the Federal lines, gained the outside of their entrenchments, and at some points a hand-to-hand conflict ensued over the top of the breastworks, the Federals beating back the Confederates with their bayonets as they attempted to climb over. Our sketch shows the repulse of the last Confederate assault.

Sheridan's Campaign In The Valley Of The Shenandoah — Fight Of Duffie's Cavalry, Near Hunter's House, Charles Town, West Virginia — Covering The Retreat Of Federal Forces.

Confederate Battery On The James River, Va., Shelling Laborers On The Dutch Gap Canal.

Our sketch, derived from a Confederate source, represents the battery which annoyed the Federal gunboats on the James River and retarded the labor on the Dutch Gap Canal. This Confederate work was situated on the upper side of the James, in almost a northerly direc- *tion from Dutch Gap. The illustration representing it is very spirited, and will enable our readers to comprehend at a glance both the character of the enterprise and the peril under which it was prosecuted. Our sketch represents the gunners at work. In the distance are seen* *the obstructions which defended the river at the end of Farrar's Island. Dutch Gap, which is more to the left, does not appear in the picture. Its position is, however, sufficiently indicated by the direction of the guns and shells.*

CHAPTER 10

TRIUMPH OF THE UNION

Sheridan Riding Along The Lines After The Battle Of Fisher's Hill, September 22d, 1864.

Ragtag And Hungry Confederates In Retreat.

AFTER THE BATTLES OF Poplar Springs Church and Hatcher's Run in the fall of 1864, Grant's forces had remained comparatively inactive in front of Richmond and Petersburg through the winter. Sheridan's victories in the Shenandoah had cut off an important source of food for the besieged Confederate capital and Petersburg, making conditions there ever more difficult for soldier and civilian alike.

Grant's position prevented a junction of Lee with Joseph Johnston. Johnston commanded the dwindling forces facing Sherman, who was driving through South Carolina, capturing Columbia on February 17, 1865. Johnston had about thirty thousand effectives, and with Lee's more than fifty thousand, their combined armies would have been formidable—although lacking equipment and supplies. Casualties would have been immense if a united Confederate force continued to resist Sherman's eighty thousand and Grant's one hundred and thirteen thousand troops. Though the situation was desperate, the Confederacy could still count on the services of top commanders such as Generals Longstreet, A. P. Hill, and Beauregard.

Late in February, Grant ordered Sheridan to destroy all of Richmond's communication lines north of the James River. With ten thousand cavalry and infantry, Sheridan defeated Early's force of two thousand at Waynesboro, then destroyed the railroad as far as Charlottesville. Next he divided his force, one part going to break up the railroad into Lynchburg, and the other to disable the James River Canal, by which the Confederate capital received a large portion of its supplies. Sheridan then rejoined the Army of the Potomac.

As the main armies prepared for a final campaign, other Federal forces were at work to seal the coming Confederate defeat. Veteran cavalry forces made raids into South Carolina and east Tennessee, destroying railroads and bridges and a vast amount of public property. In the Deep South, plans were laid for the capture of Mobile and the rest of Alabama. In March, General E. R. S. Canby, commanding the Department of the Gulf, started out against Mobile with twenty-five thousand troops. At the same time General G. H. Thomas sent thirteen thousand cavalry and two thousand infantry to cooperate with Canby and sweep down from the Tennessee River, raiding Alabama and Georgia, capturing cities and towns, and destroying more public property. ★

A Faithful Dog Watching And Defending The Dead Body Of His Confederate Master.

General James Longstreet.

Born in Edgefield, S.C., in 1821, Longstreet was an 1842 graduate of West Point and a Mexican War veteran. He served in the East and then in Tennessee, rejoining Lee for the 1864–65 campaigns in Virginia. Lee called him "my old war horse."

The Plantation Police, Or Home Guard, Examining Negro Passes On The Levee Road, Below New Orleans, La.

The Plantation Police, or Patrol, was an institution peculiar to the slave states. It was a semi-military organization, raised and supported by the planters, but recognized by the old state authorities. Their principal duty was to visit the various plantations and patrol the roads at night, arresting all Negroes and others not having proper passes. The war, the President's Emancipation Proclamation, and the actual possession of most of the State of Louisiana by the Federal authorities made these patrols doubly rigorous for a time. The colored man in the foreground seems to yield to the force of a tottering power, satisfied that his own day is at hand.

Railroad Bridge At Rappahannock Station, Va., Still Standing After Four Years Of War.

Sketches Of Army Life — Weighing Out Rations To Be Divided Among The Men.

Grant's Movements South Of The James — Battle Of Poplar Springs Church — The Ninth Corps Passing Poplar Springs Church And Confederate Prisoners Coming In, Fall Of 1864.

LEE'S LAST GAMBLES

Lee now resolved to join with Johnston to try and save their armies and fight on. He concentrated his forces near Grant's center in front of Petersburg on March 25 and made a fierce assault on Fort Stedman. Lee hoped to break through at this point, but he was unsuccessful, for Grant was prepared for the assault. Lee lost five thousand men, while Grant had about two thousand casualties.

Next, Grant moved against the Confederate right. On the morning of March 31, Sheridan advanced with cavalry and infantry and took possession of the strategic crossroads at Five Forks, while other forces went on the attack. The Confederates counterattacked to regain Five Forks, where a decisive battle was fought on April 1, with Sheridan routing his opponents.

Grant heard of this victory in his position before Petersburg, and at once ordered a bombardment along his whole line, to be kept up all night. At dawn the next morning the works of the enemy were vigorously attacked. [General H.G.] Wright with his corps managed to break through the lines, and, pushing on, drove the Confederates before him, captured a large number of guns and several thousand prisoners . . . The battle now raged furiously from right to left, the Confederates bravely fighting to hold their intrenchments. Especially determined were they to retain possession of Fort Mahone, which was defended by [A.P.] Hill's corps. In the gallant stand he made there Hill was killed.

Sheridan now came up rapidly against Lee from the west, sweeping down on the Confederate flank and rear. Richmond and Petersburg were no longer defensible, and Lee began his final retreat. Longstreet held Petersburg into the night of April 2–3 and then withdrew. ★

Blowing Out The Bulkhead Of The Dutch Gap Canal, James River, Va., January 1st, 1865.

Since August, General Butler had directed the digging of a canal near his positions at Bermuda Hundred in order to allow the passage of gunboats. Although less than two hundred yards long, the canal had to be dug under enemy fire. The work was done mainly by black troops. By January 1, the canal was to be opened by a massive explosion. At twelve minutes before four o'clock in the morning the mine was sprung, in the presence of General Butler and staff. A dense black smoke, immediately following the upheaval of the earth, was succeeded by a ponderous cloud of white smoke, which entirely filled the gap. On rolling away the smoke revealed the bank indented with a crater, into which the water ran from the canal below. No connection between the canal and the river was immediately established, however, and this work would not be completed until April.

Signaling With A Piece Of Looking Glass.

Cutting Coarse Forage Into Chaff.

Water Skin And Mode Of Carrying.

JEFFERSON DAVIS FLEES RICHMOND

On Sunday, April 2, Confederate president Jefferson Davis was attending church in Richmond, when an orderly brought him a dispatch from Lee.

With a glance he saw that all was over. He must seek safety in flight, as Richmond would soon be taken. At eight o'clock that evening he abandoned the capital and fled to Danville, to which city his wife had gone a few days before. The Confederate Congress and the Virginia Legislature also took flight.

Early the next morning, April 3, Federal troops marched into Richmond with bands playing and colors flying. The army was immediately set to work to put out the fires kindled by drunken incendiaries just after the evacuation—fires that destroyed the business part of Main Street. The Confederates left behind five thousand of their sick and wounded in the hospitals. They also left five hundred pieces of artillery, thousands of small arms, and many locomotives and cars.

When the Federal troops reached the Virginia statehouse, an officer ascended to the roof and unfurled the national flag. Richmond was once more in the hands of the United States authorities.

The news of the capture of Richmond produced great joy throughout the loyal States, for it told of the downfall of the Confederate Government. In Washington the public offices were closed; the people of New York showed their pleasure in public meetings and in the ringing of bells in the tower of Trinity Church.

Sherman, Grant, and Lincoln now met to plan the final defeat of the Confederacy. ★

Wilson's Cavalry Foraging At The Selden Estate, Clarke County, Va.

Poplar Springs Church — Charge Of The Fifth Corps On The Confederate Fort, September, 1864.

PRISONERS OF WAR

There were more than 150 military prisons in use during the war, with the disease-ridden Confederate camp at Andersonville, Georgia, the most notorious. Prisoners from both sides were confined in state penitentiaries, former military barracks, factories, warehouses, and fortresses. Conditions were harsh for men on both sides, and among the worst was Libby Prison in Richmond, where a thousand Federal officers were held in only eight rooms. Federal authorities claimed that as many as forty thousand prisoners held by the South suffered from starvation and were reduced to mere skeletons. After the war, General Lee testified that he did not know of the terrible conditions in the Confederate prisoner-of-war facilities nor even who commanded them.

Federal Cavalry Covering The Escape Of Federal Prisoners From Libby Prison, Richmond, Va.

The feeling of sympathy for the unfortunate Federal officers and men who suffered outrage in the hands of the Confederates gave way to a momentary feeling of joy as news came of the escape, at one time, of 109 officers and men. From time to time a few had escaped, and the narrative of their escapes had been among the most intensely exciting incidents of the war. But when more than a hundred contrived to get out of the Southern dungeon the interest knew no bounds. The method employed was as follows: Having managed to find access to the cellar, they commenced work, relieving one another as opportunity offered. Their instruments were case knives, pocket knives, chisels, and files. After getting through the wall they disposed of the excavated soil by drawing it out in a spittoon, which they attached to a cord. This would be filled by the party at work in the tunnel and pulled out into the cellar by their companions, who disposed of it by spreading it in shallow layers over the floor, concealing it beneath the straw. The tunnel, completed by fifty-one days of patient toil, was about sixty feet long and opened into an old tobacco shed beyond the line of guards. In order to elude their pursuers, the fugitives scattered as much as possible. Many were their hardships and sufferings, and frequent were their narrow escapes from the Confederate cavalry, who the next morning were bushwhacking in every direction for them. The joy which these escapees experienced when they first caught sight of the Federals cannot be expressed.

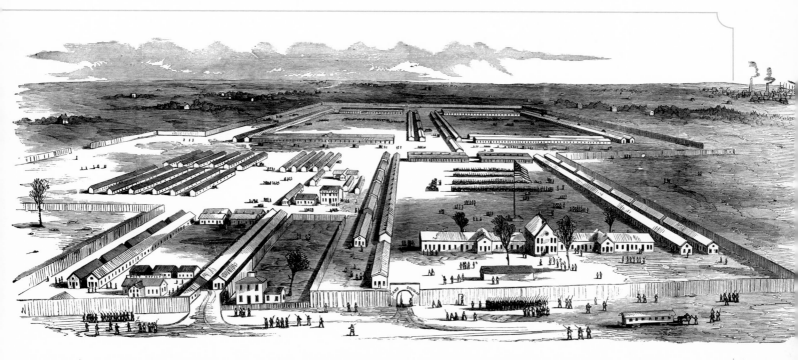

Bird's-eye View Of Camp Douglas, Chicago, Ill., Used For The Detention Of Confederate Prisoners.

View Of Richmond From The Prison Camp At Belle Isle, James River.

Belle Isle, situated in the James River, is about an acre and a half, and in this small space ten thousand Federal soldiers were imprisoned. The Confederate capital is in the distance beyond the railroad bridge.

Sherman's Seventeenth Corps Crossing The South Edisto River, S. C., February 9th, 1865.

SHERMAN'S CONQUEST

Campaigning through late winter of 1865, Sherman brought his opponents to the brink of defeat. In February he took Charleston, that symbol of rebellion, which had been abandoned that month without further action.

A few weeks afterward Major Anderson celebrated the anniversary of his evacuation of Fort Sumter four years before by raising over the ruins of that fortress the same flag which he had been compelled to haul down then, and which he had carried away with him.

Next, Sherman passed into North Carolina, defeating a force of twenty thousand Confederates under General W.J. Hardee at Averasborough on March 16. Two days later, near Bentonville, Sherman was surprised by an attack from Johnston's army.

There was a terrible battle. Six times did the [Confederates] fall fiercely upon the Federals, and nothing but the most desperate efforts saved Sherman's army from destruction. His troops made a brave stand, and at length succeeded in gaining the victory, the Confederates retreating to Raleigh, the capital of North Carolina.

Sherman massed his entire force at Goldsborough, knowing Johnston would fight on stubbornly and try to unite with Lee. ★

Sherman's "Bummers" Foraging and Robbing Homes In South Carolina.

Our artist sent us with this sketch of "Bummers Foraging" a graphic account of their modus operandi. He wrote: "These active and unscrupulous fellows generally started out every morning mounted on very mean horseflesh, and as a general rule they always came back very well mounted. The horses they had ridden in the morning were now pack animals, laden with all the good things of this world. In one place in South Carolina they came to a large plantation owned by a leading Confederate named Fitzgerald. Here the Federal soldiers found, buried in various out-of-the-way places, an immense quantity of gold and silver plate, of the aggregate value of over $70,000; here they also found a large quantity of the finest Madeira wine, which had been stowed away in the old gentleman's wine cellar for nearly thirty years. Indeed, it may be said that these brave fellows had plenty of good wine to drink on their memorable march through Georgia and South Carolina."

REGIMENTAL FLAGS

On the stripes of this flag of the 84th Regiment of Infantry, United States Colored Troops, are names of the regiment's campaigns, including the service in the Gulf region. Regimental flags that were carried into battle often were so torn from bullets that new flags were made and inscribed with the unit's exploits. Flags, usually of silk, generally were received from civilian associations close to the regiment. After the war, even the most tattered battle flags— sometimes only a piece of the staff remaining—were officially and fondly placed in storage at the regiment's state capital.

Flag of the 84th Regiment of Infantry

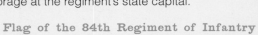

Seacoast Operations Against Charleston — Brilliant Dash And Capture Of Confederate Rifle Pits And Prisoners By The Federal Troops On James Island, S. C., February 9th, 1865.

The Old Flag Again On Sumter — Raised (On A Temporary Staff Formed Of An Oar And Boathook) By Captain H. M. Bragg, Of General Gillmore's Staff, February 18th, 1865.

Battle Near Kinston, N. C., March 8th, 1865.

APPOMATTOX

Sheridan's cavalry led the pursuit, preventing Lee's southward retreat along a railroad line. Lee's position was ever more desperate. From Amelia Court House he swung to the west but found his way once more blocked at Farmville. Grant wrote to him:

"The result of the last week must convince you of the hopelessness of further resistance . . . I regard it as my duty to shift from myself the responsibility of any further effusion of blood by asking of you the surrender of that portion of the Confederate States Army known as the Army of Northern Virginia." In his reply to this Lee . . . reciprocated the desire to avoid useless effusion of blood; "and therefore," he added, "before considering your proposition I ask the terms you will offer on condition of its surrender."

As Lee resumed withdrawing toward the mountains near Lynchburg, the two commanders exchanged messages. On the morning of April 9, Palm Sunday, Lee was repulsed in an attempt to break through Sheridan's lines near Appomattox Court House, and at last accepted surrender terms, signed later that day.

It was agreed that Lee and his officers should give their parole of honor not to take arms against the Government of the United States until properly exchanged; that the officers were to be allowed to keep their side arms, baggage and private horses, and that the officers and men would not be disturbed by United States authorities so long as they should observe their parole and the laws in force where they should reside. On Wednesday, April 12th, the Confederates laid down their arms and departed for their homes. ★

General Ambrose P. Hill.

Born in Culpeper County, Va., in 1825, Hill graduated West Point in 1847 and served in Mexico. A key corps commander throughout the war, he was killed in the defense of Petersburg, Va., on April 2, 1865.

SOLDIER'S HOUSEWIFE
The items essential to comfort in camp included a sewing kit known as a "soldier's housewife," a twist of tobacco, a coffee bag and pot, and a lamp and stove.

Camp Life — Chimney Architecture — The Federal Soldiers At Their Camp Fires.

The Campaign On The James River — General Butler Landing At Fort Pawhatan.

President Lincoln Riding Through Richmond, Va., April 4th, 1865, Amid Enthusiastic Cheers.

JOY AND SORROW

Just before 10 p.m. on April 14, 1865, President Lincoln was seated with his wife and friends in a box at Washington's Ford Theater, when Confederate sympathizer John Wilkes Booth entered and shot him in the back of the head.

Shouting "Sic semper tyrannis!"—"So may it always be with tyrants"—and "The South is avenged!" the assassin leaped down to the stage and fled.

On the same night that the President was shot Secretary of State [William H.] Seward was stabbed and badly wounded by an accomplice of Booth, which gave rise to a belief that a plot had been arranged for the murder of the President, all the members of the Cabinet, General Grant and others.

Several persons were arrested, and their trial resulted in convictions and executions. Booth was pursued to a barn near Fredericksburg and was shot dead.

Andrew Johnson was sworn in as seventeenth

General Ulysses S. Grant.

Born in Ohio in 1822, Grant graduated West Point in 1843, undistinguished as a cadet. Cited for gallantry in the Mexican War, he left the army in 1854. He commanded an Illinois regiment at the start of the Civil War, rising swiftly with repeated battlefield success. As General in Chief of the Armies of the United States after March 1864, he directed the overall strategy until war's end. Grant was elected president in 1868 and served two terms.

president of the United States. On April 17 Sherman arranged the surrender of Johnston's army of twenty-five thousand men. Meanwhile, Jefferson Davis was fleeing toward the Gulf of Mexico, pursued by Federal cavalry.

[They] left no stone unturned to find him. They soon discovered his whereabouts, and at early dawn [on May 10] approached the camp where he was resting for the night, from opposite directions. Mistaking each other for enemies, both opened fire, and thus aroused the sleepers. Davis tried to make his escape disguised in a woman's waterproof cloak and a shawl thrown over his head . . . but he was detected and captured.

Davis was taken to Fortress Monroe and imprisoned under an indictment for treason. He was never tried, and after two years he was released, at liberty until his death in 1889. ★

Voluntary Dispersion Of Kirby Smith's Confederate Army At Shreveport, La., May 23d, 1865.

The Soldier's Rest — Friends Of The Seventh And Eighth Regiments, New York Volunteers, Welcoming The Return Of Their Heroes Carrying Tattered Battle Flags.

The Grand Review At Washington, D.C., May 24th, 1865 — President Johnson, Lieutenant General Grant, And Others Inspecting Sherman's Army — Sherman Saluting At The Head Of His Staff.

GRANT'S FAREWELL TO THE TROOPS

The Civil War was over, and in celebration one hundred and fifty thousand Union soldiers paraded through Washington on May 23–24, 1865.

A grand, imposing spectacle was presented when the brave soldiers who had endured hardships and risked their lives for the preservation of the Union returned from the field of battle to go back to their peaceful avocations . . . A beautiful close to the terrible struggle they had passed through was the grand review in Washington of the two armies that had conquered Lee and Johnston.

On June 2, General-in-Chief Grant issued an address to give thanks to the men before they all were mustered out of the army:

Soldiers of the Armies of the United States: By your patriotic devotion to your country in the hour of danger and alarm, and your magnificent fighting, bravery and endurance, you have maintained the supremacy of the Union and the Constitution, overthrown all armed opposition to the enforcement of the laws and of the proclamation forever abolishing slavery—the cause and pretext of the rebellion—and opened the way to the rightful authorities to restore order and inaugurate peace on a permanent and enduring basis on every foot of American soil . . . To achieve these glorious triumphs, and secure to yourselves, your fellow countrymen and posterity the blessings of free institutions, tens of thousands of your gallant comrades have fallen, and sealed the priceless legacy with their blood. The graves of these a grateful nation bedews with tears. It honors their memories, and will ever cherish and support their stricken families. ★

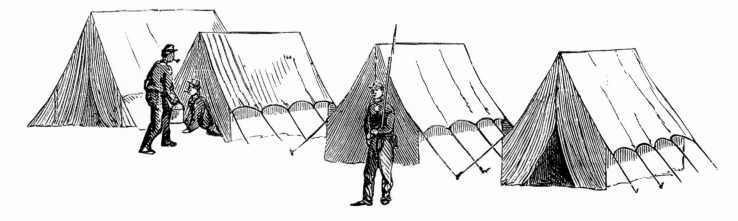

PICTURE CREDITS

The following abbreviation is used:
NMAH/SI—National Museum of American History, Behring Center, Smithsonian Institution. (Smithsonian Institution negative numbers appear in brackets.)

Frontispiece The cover of *Frank Leslie's Illustrated History of the Civil War,* 1895 edition. **viii**t Frank Leslie; Library of Congress **viii**b Mrs. Frank Leslie; Library of Congress

Chapter 1: A Nation in Crisis 5t Armed Forces History, Division of History of Technology, NMAH/SI [2004-22494.03a] **8**bl Armed Forces History, Division of History of Technology, NMAH/SI [2002-3852.02] **8**br Armed Forces History, Division of History of Technology, NMAH/SI [2004-56148] **11**t Numismatics, Division of Information Technology & Science, NMAH/SI [2004-54117] **15**t Armed Forces History, Division of History of Technology, NMAH/SI [2003-8944] **15**r Armed Forces History, Division of History of Technology, NMAH/SI [2004-40534] **19**b Armed Forces History, Division of History of Technology, NMAH/SI [2001-4081] **21**tl Armed Forces History, Division of History of Technology, NMAH/SI [2004-19156.07a] **21**tr Armed Forces History, Division of History of Technology, NMAH/SI [2004-19157.08a] **21**cr Armed Forces History, Division of History of Technology, NMAH/SI [2004-19157.06a]

Chapter 2: North and South at War 29t Physical Science, Division of Science, Medicine & Society, NMAH/SI [2004-55790] **31**tr Armed Forces History, Division of History of Technology, NMAH/SI [78-1080] **33**t Armed Forces History, Division of History of Technology, NMAH/SI [2001-4032] **38**tl Armed Forces History, Division of History of Technology, NMAH/SI [2004-40508] **38**tr Armed Forces History, Division of History of Technology, NMAH/SI [2004-51711] **43**t Armed Forces History, Division of History of Technology, NMAH/SI [2004-22554.04] **43**c Armed Forces History, Division of History of Technology, NMAH/SI [2004-22554.01]

Chapter 3: 'On to Richmond' 48tr Armed Forces History, Division of History of Technology, NMAH/SI [2004-20299] **55**tr Armed Forces History, Division of History of Technology, NMAH/SI [2004-22553.03] **58**cl Armed Forces History, Division of History of Technology, NMAH/SI [2004-51192] **59**tl Armed Forces History, Division of History of Technology, NMAH/SI [2004-51191]

Chapter 4: Lee in Command 73br Armed Forces History, Division of History of Technology, NMAH/SI [2004-39194.03] **78**b Armed Forces History, Division of History of Technology, NMAH/SI [2004-26286.06] **81**t Division of Cultural History, NMAH/SI [2001-7973] **85**b Armed Forces History, Division of History of Technology, NMAH/SI [2004-47038] **89**b Armed Forces History, Division of History of Technology, NMAH/SI [2004-51190]

Chapter 5: War on River and Coast 94bl Armed Forces History, Division of History of Technology, NMAH/SI [2002-3867.10]

Chapter 6: The Northern Tide Rises 127tr Armed Forces History, Division of History of Technology, NMAH/SI [2004-53680]

Chapter 7: Insurrection, Siege, and Union Advance 137bl Armed Forces History, Division of History of Technology, NMAH/SI [2004-47039] **137**br Armed Forces History, Division of History of Technology, NMAH/SI [2004-47040] **140**tr Armed Forces History, Division of History of Technology, NMAH/SI [2004-30636]

Chapter 8: The Confederacy Fights On 155b Armed Forces History, Division of History of Technology, NMAH/SI [2001-4019] **157**tl Armed Forces History, Division of History of Technology, NMAH/SI [2004-26285.02] **157**tr Armed Forces History, Division of History of Technology, NMAH/SI [2004-46234] **159**br Armed Forces History, Division of History of Technology, NMAH/SI [2001-3998]

Chapter 9: Grant's Relentless Assaults 178b Armed Forces History, Division of History of Technology, NMAH/SI [2001-4026]

Chapter 10: Triumph of the Union 202tr Armed Forces History, Division of History of Technology, NMAH/SI [82-7776] **206**bl Armed Forces History, Division of History of Technology, NMAH/SI [2004-51990]

A Selection of *Leslie's* Maps 212l Armed Forces History, Division of History of Technology, NMAH/SI [2004-47032] **212**c Armed Forces History, Division of History of Technology, NMAH/SI [2004-47034]